Ferrarin

# PARENTING WITH AN ATTITUDE

## *21 Questions Successful Parents Ask Themselves*

By

## Ed Wimberly, Ph.D.

THOUGHTS AND IDEAS FOR GOOD PARENTS
WHO WANT TO BE BETTER PARENTS

Parenting with an Attitude . . . *21 Questions Successful Parents Ask Themselves*

© 2008 Ed Wimberly, Ph.D.

JOURNEY BOOKS

ISBN: 978-1-4276-3225-8

To order a copy of *Parenting with an Attitude*, go to www.raisinggreatkids.com

Cover graphics and design by Kim Hansen—www.hansendesignhouse.com

# *Dedication*

To my wife, Joan, who has taught me more about life, love and parenting than I could have ever learned in scores of lifetimes with anyone else. Thank you.

And to my absolutely great daughters, Ashley and Allyson, both of whom have been the source of unlimited joy and happiness. I miss being the father of two little girls—it was fun (most of the time!) while it lasted. But as fulfilling as that time was with you both, I enjoy and treasure this season of just being your friend even more. Thank you.

And to my mom who provided me with a quiet, humble, and yet wise model of what it takes to be a good parent. Thank you, Mom.

# Contents

# Introduction

SOMEONE ONCE SAID (I'M not sure, but I think it might have been my mother!), that a newborn baby is the only "new product" on the market today that, once we get it home and find that it leaks at both ends, we can't return it for a refund. Even though we can't—and don't really want to—down deep, that is exactly what most of us parents have wanted to at one time or another.

Like it or not—and I believe that it is perfectly normal to not like it at times—we all have the honor, responsibility, and privilege of taking our new product, that is far from perfect and complete, and applying our influences to create a healthy, responsible, productive human being. With no instruction manual provided, it is natural that most parents feel overwhelmed and inadequate at the thought of completing "the assembly process."

New born babies do not come "programmed" with so much of what they will need to navigate their world, so we parents are assigned the task of developing and nurturing virtues such as self control, independence, healthy self-esteem, values, morals, and a sense of responsibility. Because we are their parents, it is our job to make sure that these and many other qualities and characteristics are in place and activated in their lives before they leave our home and our care. Accomplishing all that is required of us parents, helping develop our "unfinished product" is what *Parenting with an Attitude* is all about.

There will be no easy answers or simple solutions provided here. In fact, at times, you might even be frustrated because you will be encouraged to look more at yourself and your attitudes as a parent, than at your kids and their attitudes and behaviors. And I cannot assure you that all of your questions will be answered, or that this book will address everything you need to know to raise kids who are healthy and free of chronic anger. But I *can* assure you that you will come away with a new perspective that will help you to be the best parent to your kids that you can possibly be.

I can hear the skeptics now: "Yeah right! All I have to do is follow the 'recipe' found in this guy's book and all my fears and problems as a parent will cease to exist! Nothing can be that easy!"

I would agree. The skeptics are right. Nothing—especially being the kind of parent your kids need—can be that easy. There is no simple formula to replace the good old fashioned hard work and sacrifice required of parents. My purpose is not to make parenting easy but rather, to make good parenting a possibility. As parents entering the twenty first century, there have never been more distractions and temptations that threaten to pull kids in the wrong direction. Parents need help to raise kids who are healthy, free of anger, and empowered to become emotionally prosperous adults. *Parenting with an Attitude* is full of ideas, concepts, and suggestions that will swing the odds of being successful parents back to your favor. Mistakes will still be made (I know that all too well first hand), but if you consider the concepts of this book, you will significantly increase the chances of raising emotionally healthy kids.

## ATTITUDE VS. APPROACH

*Parenting with an Attitude* takes a different direction than do many of the parenting books on the market today. Most address the goals and expectations good parents should have for their kids, and usually these books are written to endorse a particular parenting approach to accomplish such goals. But the primary purpose of this book is to guide you as a parent to assess and evaluate what attitudes you have toward and about your kids and to see how those attitudes either enable you to be a successful parent, or how they interfere with your efforts.

Successful parenting is more about attitude than it is approach. Of course it is important to have goals and expectations for your kids. And certainly to reach and accomplish those goals, it is usually necessary that we use and apply approaches that will help us. But rather than focusing solely on shaping their behaviors to be what we expect them to be, it is important that we parents also evaluate our own attitudes which we carry into our relationships with our children.

I have seldom run across a parent who disagrees with the notion that the attitudes we have about and toward our kids play a very important role in our ability to be an influence in their lives—but all too often, the importance of attitude is minimized and even ignored in our role as parents. As an author, therapist and dad of two wonderful girls, I have found that it is only when we examine our own attitudes that we are then able to choose the most effective parenting approaches. And only then can we "design" kids who are healthy, well balanced, and free of self-defeating, destructive personality characteristics.

In this book, you will be encouraged to look at yourself and your role as a parent. This self-assessment will help fine-tune your attitudes, and as a result, be better equipped to pick and choose the most effective parenting approaches for you and your family. The foundational question to ask is this: what attitudes do I have toward and about my kids, and do those attitudes help or hinder me in my efforts to raise a healthy child, free of anger? Certainly the approaches and techniques you use to correct, challenge, encourage, and discipline are of great importance. But without healthy and appropriate attitudes as a backdrop, all of the best approaches and intentions will likely fall short.

## THE IMPORTANCE OF SELF-ESTEEM

Developing self-esteem in our kids is an important goal, the success of which relies heavily on the attitudes we have about them. In our society, the term "self-esteem" is often over used and misused, but the fact is: kids who grow up with a clear and balanced estimate of their worth and value have a much better shot at growing into healthy and well adjusted adults. Likewise, kids who are constantly wondering where they fit—if indeed they fit at all—will have a more difficult time coping with the many pitfalls and struggles they will face in life.

When it comes to self-esteem and children, I have become convinced of three principles that this book is based on. First, the truly happy and healthy kids in this world are not necessarily the ones who have fewer struggles; nor are they those with the greatest opportunities. The healthiest and happiest kids are the fortunate ones who know how to deal effectively with life's struggles. And it is a strong sense of their own value and worth that will help give them the ability to cope and deal well with the "curve balls" in life that are sure to come their way.

Secondly, kids deserve to feel good about themselves. And the basis for their self-esteem is seldom how pretty or handsome they are. Their worth should not even be based on the fact that they are intelligent or living up to parental expectations. Kids deserve to feel good about themselves simply because they are—just because they exist. This does not mean that when they blow it, that you won't be disappointed or hurt or even angry; that too, is part of parenting. These negative reactions from you or even from themselves at times, are indeed inevitable. The key is that such occasional negative responses must not break their spirit, or take away from their feeling that they have value and worth to you just because they are.

The third principle is this: How kids view themselves is designed. It doesn't just happen, it's not genetically predetermined, and it's not the luck of the draw. It is learned, and in large part, it is learned through you and your efforts to design how it is they grow up feeling about themselves.

## A PARENT'S ROLE IN DEVELOPING SELF-ESTEEM

As parents, our influence on our children's self-esteem comes through our interactions with them and our messages to them about how we view and value them. Most often the messages we send to our kids are subtle and can even be subconscious at times. But nonetheless, our messages to them help shape their view of themselves over a period of time.

Several years ago, I had the opportunity to observe the parenting skills of a mom and dad who had an office next to mine. During the time that I knew them both, their son would often spend time in their office after school and on the weekends. Every time he came, I became increasingly impressed with how they talked with their 10-year-old son, how they responded to him, answered his questions, how they disciplined him, and how they treated him with the same respect and equality they expected from him.

I don't typically make it a habit of commenting on the parenting skills of others; I have always assumed that if anyone wanted my opinion, they would ask for it. In this case however, I decided that this very impressive mom and dad would not mind if I told them what a good job I thought they were doing with their son. After complimenting them, the mom smiled and said that they often received comments on their son's good behavior. Invariably, she related, the comments usually went something like this: "You are so fortunate to have such an easy child."

She went on to say that for the longest time she was a bit ir-ritated by such compliments because they implied that they were simply "lucky" for giving birth to an easy child, with little regard for the possibility that their parenting efforts had something to do with it. One day it occurred to her to respond by smiling and say-ing, "Thanks. We designed him that way."

A point well taken since in fact they had, to some degree, de-signed him to be an "easy child." Certainly genetics, predisposition and other factors come into play but the parental influence played a large part in designing a child's disposition.

*Parenting with an Attitude* is about how we parents can com-municate with our kids in such a way that will help them become adults who are free of anger and who possess a healthy self-esteem. This task is not an easy one, and there are no guarantees. The in-fluence we have—while incredibly strong and significant—is only one factor in determining how our children will develop and grow; how they evolve and mature is not completely in a parent's hands. Other factors, from genetic predisposition to peer pressure enter the mix as powerful influences.

It is also important to note, that as our kids grow they must take responsibility for their actions and their choices. Our chil-dren are not solely the product of our mistakes any more than they are the product of our efforts and successes; rather, they are more a product of how they choose to respond, to both our suc-cesses and our failures.

However, since we are the first influence in their lives, and during the early years when they are so extremely moldable, the messages they receive from us are crucial. We have the benefit of a head start in being an influence and impact in their lives, well before all the other forces that will soon bombard them come on the scene. This book is written to insure that your impact is posi-tive and constructive, and that your early influence continues for a lifetime.

## KIDS DON'T NEED PERFECT PARENTS

As I wrote about raising healthy kids, I was confronted more than once by my own imperfections as a parent. At times it was painful recalling my own flaws. But then, over and over I was reminded of how absolutely great (not perfect, but great) our two daughters, Ashley and Allyson, have turned out—in spite of any shortcomings and mistakes Joan and I made. I believe this is due to the fact that we were always working hard to put into practice the principles outlined in this book.

So I encourage you to set aside any perfectionist tendencies you might have and remember that your kids do not need you to be a perfect parent. However, hey *do* need you to love them, and to consistently work at keeping your parenting attitudes on the right track. It is my hope that the following principles and suggestions will help you accomplish this very difficult but exciting task.

In order to help you assess and evaluate your attitudes about parenting, I am suggesting 21 questions for you to consider—each of which is important for every parent to contemplate along their journey to raise healthy and happy kids. At the end of each chapter you will find discussion questions to further assist you in evaluating your attitudes about parenting and your kids.

## DOES THE BIBLE OFFER US PARENTS ANY HELP?

The Bible provides many of us with a guide to everyday living. And whether or not you consider its writing to have been inspired by God, it provides a great deal of wisdom and insight for parents who want to be the best they can be.

Psalms 119:105 (NIV) tells us that the Scriptures were written to, "be a lamp unto your feet and a light unto your path." It seems reasonable to assume then, that this promise includes lighting "the path" of parenthood and that the Bible has a lot to offer parents searching for guidance.

I know most parents would like to find even more in the Scriptures—like an edict about which specific parenting philosophies to subscribe to. I for one would have welcomed a very clear and concise recipe for what approaches we could have used in all of the many situations and circumstances that came our way while my wife and I were raising our two daughters.

Should we spank or not spank? What's the best approach to use when Allyson spills her milk for the third time at one meal? How should we handle Ashley's grumpy mood? What's the best response to a rebellious spirit? Should we count when we are telling them to do something and they are dragging their feet? And if we do count, is counting to three enough, or should we count to 10? Maybe we should count to 20 if we want to be really patient? Just how patient should we be?

A recipe or two from the Bible—or any source for that matter—would certainly help take the guesswork out of parenting wouldn't it?

But what you'll find in the Scriptures is not a recipe for what your *approach* should be but rather, a guide to what *attitudes* are important to have in order to be a successful parent. I believe there are at least three good reasons for this emphasis on attitude over approach in the Bible.

First, there are few parenting approaches that will universally work well and consistently, regardless of the child or the offense. As parents, it is our responsibility to use our wisdom to determine what approaches are most suitable for all of the many circumstances that we'll face. It is impossible for any book to give us an absolute and universal approach to apply to all kids and all situations.

Secondly, when our attitudes toward our kids are right and appropriate, then the most effective approach is more likely to follow.

Finally, when our attitudes toward our kids are not right, then any approach we might use is likely to be ineffective in the long run.

So the Bible serves as a guide to better parenting by helping us fine-tune our attitudes toward our kids, rather than offering specific approaches for us to use.

When I speak to parent groups, I usually begin by asking those present what they think the Bible has to say about being a successful and effective parent. There are several scripture references that seem to consistently dominate their responses:

Proverbs: 22:6 (NIV): "Train up a child in the way he should go and when he is old, he will not turn from it."

Proverbs 23:13-14 (NIV): "Do not withhold discipline from a child. If you punish him with a rod he will not die."

Proverbs 29:17(NIV): "Discipline your son, and he will give you peace; he will bring delight to your soul."

And the usual favorite and most quoted by parents:

Colossians 3:20 (NIV): "Children obey your parents in everything, for this pleases the Lord." For some strange reason, this particular verse seems to be the favorite of most of us parents!

Certainly, these verses are invaluable Biblical directives that, when applied, will help us to be more effective parents. But as relevant as these suggestions are, there are two additional verses that are quite possibly the most important and foundational to parenting, and yet, often overlooked and minimized in their importance and relevance to parenting.

## AVOIDING ANGER AND BITTERNESS IN OUR KIDS

Ephesians 6:4 (NIV): "Avoid provoking your children to anger."

Colossians 3:21: "Do not embitter your children or they will become discouraged."

On occasion a parent will acknowledge that not provoking their child to anger is indeed an important Biblical guideline. It is likely, however, to be mentioned last and least emphasized as an important goal. Usually their explanation for minimizing this Biblical directive is that they feel it is virtually impossible to avoid anger in their kids. As a responsible parent—so the explanation goes—they have rules, expectations and standards to which they hold their kids accountable. Their kids often become angry in response to their restrictions and expectations. Anger in their kids is simply unavoidable.

And I would agree. Not only is avoiding anger in our kids impossible, it might even be said, that to do so entirely would require our consistently giving in to them in order to avoid their anger. This is not an option that any responsible parent would consider.

## Chronic anger vs. transient anger

I refer to this inevitable anger in kids resulting from healthy and appropriate parental authority as "transient anger," and it should not be confused with the anger the Bible encourages parents to avoid. Certainly, it is understandable as well as unavoidable that all children will experience transient anger toward their parents from time to time—for limiting them, challenging them, and holding them accountable. It is only natural for children to not always (or not *ever* when they are teenagers!) appreciate parental rules, regulations and expectations. And anger is often the inevitable and natural result.

Ephesians 6:4 and Colossians 3:21 however, relate to the chronic anger and bitterness in kids that is likely to develop when parents foster unhealthy and unacceptable attitudes toward them.

This book is written for the express purpose of helping parents appraise and evaluate the attitudes they have toward their kids. In turn, they will be more able to minimize the likelihood of raising kids who grow up to be angry and bitter adults. Should you find that a change or adjustment in your attitudes is necessary, there are suggestions here that may help in your efforts at raising kids who are not scarred by unnecessary, chronic and destructive anger and bitterness.

Finally, I would encourage you to take advantage of the discussion questions that are at the end of each of the 21 chapters. Use these questions to stimulate conversation between you and others as a way of more fully understanding what your attitudes toward your kids are. And as you are using the discussion questions to stimulate your thinking about your parenting attitudes, you might also find value in using them to look back on your own childhood experiences with your parents.

I hope you will enjoy what you are about to read and that it will have a positive influence on your parenting efforts.

*Ed Wimberly*

# 21 Questions Successful Parents Ask Themselves

Most parents would acknowledge that they are always looking for answers. Too often we are unable to find the answers we need because we are not asking the right questions. Rather than asking the typical questions (Where have we gone wrong? Why won't Austin ever listen? Why can't my kids be as well behaved as the neighbor's kids? Why do they always want to be at someone else's house? Why me?), I will address some of the more important questions that parents must ask themselves if they are to find answers that can be of help to them.

The first thing you will notice about the 21 questions suggested here is that they all focus primarily on you and what you can do, rather than on your kids and how they should change. I have always believed that if we want to see growth in our kids, we must first look at ourselves and what part we might be playing in perpetuating and reinforcing (not causing, but encouraging) the very behavior or attitudes that we dislike. As you evaluate and fine tune your attitudes, you will likely not only see growth in your kids, but in your relationship with them as well.

As you consider these 21 questions, I would also challenge you to focus on your own childhood, and to re-examine your relationship with your own parents and the attitudes they had toward you. Often, a great deal can be learned about how you parent by exploring how you were parented.

*"What our kids hear us say about them helps create a road map for how they see themselves and what they decide they have to offer as human beings."*

# Question #1:

## *What do my kids hear me say about them?*

UNLIKE AN ADULT'S BRAIN, the brain of a young child resembles a sponge, absorbing as truth what it hears, what it is told, and what it experiences. As such, during the early years of development young brains are unable to think and process like an adult. While not impossible, it becomes difficult for children to reject or discard in the future what it absorbed during those early and most vulnerable years of development.

Suppose someone said to you, "You are so clumsy." Since you have a fully developed adult brain that is capable of processing feedback from the outside world, you are able to absorb that feedback and either accept or reject their opinion. You are capable of both taking in the fact that this person thinks you are clumsy, and of deciding for yourself whether or not you agree.

In addition to having a brain that is physically developed, you have also accumulated life experiences, observations and feedback from others regarding your dexterity: "I agree. I am a clumsy person. What they are telling me fits with what I have been told by others, and what I have observed myself." Or you are able to disagree: "You are wrong. I am not a clumsy person. Your input is inconsistent with what I have observed and been told about my own dexterity. So thank you, but I respectfully disagree."

Consider the influence we have over the conclusions our kids come to about themselves in another way. There is really only one reason we all universally refer to that object with a light bulb in it as a "lamp." Early on, over and over again, we heard everyone around us referring to it as a lamp. Slowly but ever so surely (because our sponge-like brain absorbed it), we concluded that, "the object sitting on the table with a bulb in it seems to always be called a lamp, so that's what I will call it too." And once we connected the object to the label, it became very difficult to change.

In the same way that our children draw conclusions about the tens of thousands of objects around them as a result of what they hear from others, so too do they come to conclusions about themselves. In a sense, we have all been "brainwashed" to assign labels to the countless objects that make up our environment. And while we do not usually think of brainwashing in positive terms, it is necessary and can either be used for good, or it can create lifelong scars. Imagine how confusing and disorganized our efforts to communicate with each other would be if we had not all been brainwashed to assign consistent labels to the objects around us? Communication as we know it would be virtually impossible.

Likewise, our kids will either set out in life to live up to or to live down the messages they have heard from us. The question we must consider regarding this process of early childhood "brainwashing" is this: do we use it in a good and effective fashion—and with healthy motivations—or do we use it in such a way that shapes our kids to think less of themselves? Young children are vulnerable to everything they see and hear because the conclusions they come to about themselves during their early years, will set the course for the rest of their lives.

This tendency to either live up to, or to live down, early childhood messages and expectations, helps explain how it is that parents have the power to shape their children's lives for years to come. It also provides an insight as to why many children and adults alike are drawn to similar and familiar unhealthy relationships, and in so doing, maintain a consistent life pattern of failure.

Likewise, it helps explain why those who received healthy and realistic messages about themselves, tend to gravitate toward people who also have a healthy perspective about themselves and life in general. Whoever first uttered the words, "Birds of a feather flock together," was right.

The animal world provides another example of how the conclusions and decisions children make about themselves can last a lifetime. Animal researchers took a small fish tank and placed a piece of glass down the middle. On one side, they placed an eel and one of its favorite snacks, a small shrimp. On the other side, and out of the eel's reach, they put a much larger quantity of shrimp. It doesn't take an expert in animal research to know that the shrimp placed on the same side as the eel was immediately eaten. Then the eel proceeded to go after the shrimp on the other side of the glass. The researchers waited to see what would happen. The eel—time and time again—ran into the glass in an attempt to reach and eat the remaining shrimp. Of course, each attempt led to failure. The eel—no doubt sporting a major headache—eventually gave up. It no longer tried to get the shrimp, because with each failed attempt it had become increasingly convinced, that it was impossible to reach the shrimp. "Why even try?" must have been the reasoning of the very frustrated eel.

This behavior was not surprising, but what happened next baffled the researchers. After the eel had given up all hope of reaching the shrimp, the glass barrier was removed. To their surprise, the eel continued in its passive, what's-the-use behavior, even though it could have made a quick and satisfying meal of the shrimp in an instant. The eel had given up, and although it was surrounded by its favorite meal, no further attempts were made to eat the shrimp.

All of this to say, there is bad news, but then there is also good news about how we parents will inevitably influence our kids by the messages we give them about themselves.

## FIRST, THE BAD NEWS

The bad news is that our kids, with their sponge-like brains, are not unlike the eel in this experiment. "Tyler, you're so clumsy!" Tyler's internal and undetectable response is: "Oh, so that's what I am! So, that's how they see me, and how they expect me to act!" Because of Tyler's undeveloped brain and his limited life experience, the comments of his parents become expectations for him to live down. Stated simply, a parent's negative comments—when heard repeatedly—become a self-fulfilling prophecy that could shape a child for a lifetime.

Even the best of parents can forget that kids have ears that work, even when they don't seem to be tuned in to adult conversations. Even when it does not appear to us that they are paying attention to our conservations, their little sponge-like brains are absorbing most of what they are hearing:

To the neighbor: "Kirsten is just like her mom, clumsy and awkward!"

To the teacher: "Courtney never seems to listen to instructions. Her mind seems to always be somewhere else."

To the babysitter: "You've really got your hands full tonight!"

To your best friend: "It seems like every day Matthew is more and more like my ex-husband."

All of these comments and others like them can lead kids to the many conclusions they come to about themselves. Our comments may seem harmless; they may even appear to be ignored by our kids, but over time they can have a devastating cumulative impact. And then it is more likely than not that they will set out in life to live down those negative expectations to which they've grown accustomed. Like it or not, we are in a position to limit and shape our kids in ways that interfere with the development of their full potential. We have the influence and power to manipulate their sponge-like brains to think, feel, and believe less about themselves. That's bad news.

## AND THEN, THE GOOD NEWS

The good news—and it is very good news indeed—is that parents are also in a position to be a constructive and positive influence. Just as they hear and are likely to respond to our negative messages, our kids are just as likely to react to the positive expectations and messages they hear from us. What a child hears, observes, and absorbs can either benefit their self-esteem and development, or those messages will undermine and wound their sense of worth and value.

## WHAT'S A PARENT TO DO?

Compare the previous negative comments with the following positive comments:

To the grandparents: "I really enjoy bringing Nathan to the store with me. He is usually a big help and fun to be with, too."

To her teacher: "Amber is working hard at school and I am sure that it will soon pay off with better grades."

To the babysitter: "Zac has had a hard day, but we've had a talk and I am sure you can count on him to cooperate with you while we are gone."

To your best friend: "Having Bradley in our lives the past twelve years has brought us so much happiness."

To his dad: "I always knew Matthew could do it!"

These are but a few of the many simple messages our kids hear from us that over time, will help shape the view they have of themselves. It's not brain surgery in terms of the difficulty of the task, but for many parents, it just doesn't always come naturally. Hopefully these examples will help.

## What's the bottom line?

It is inevitable that the expectations we have for our kids will become their first and most significant road map for developing a sense of who they are and what they have to offer the world. Having absorbed what they have observed, heard and concluded about what we expect them to be, they then set out in life to perpetuate what they heard about themselves as kids.

Since childhood patterns, both healthy and unhealthy, tend to continue throughout their lives, giving our kids positive and healthy expectations to live up to is essential. Our words, messages, and attitudes—as well as our physical expressions—will either convey messages and expectations that will shape, mold and encourage them to think well of themselves, or contribute to their becoming self-doubting adults who are less prepared to deal with life and the struggles that will come their way from time to time.

## DISCUSSION QUESTIONS:

1.  What is one message you consistently heard as a child that you are either living up to, or down to?

2.  In what way does that early childhood message you heard affect you in any way today?

3.  What are some of the messages you are sending your kids that are shaping and influencing their conclusions regarding themselves?

4.  What is the most common message your kids hear from you regarding them?

5.  What affect does that message currently seem to be having on them?

6.  How is that consistent message from you likely shaping how they will be as adults?

*"Kids who are respected by their parents are more likely to show respect toward others."*

# Question #2:

## *Do I respect my kids?*

THE SUGGESTION THAT IT IS IMPORTANT for parents to respect their kids is a notion for which some may not have much tolerance. Before you dismiss it as some wild and hair-brained idea from a liberal and permissive parent, please hear me out.

There are usually only two broad and compelling motivations that will lead us to obey and cooperate with someone who has authority over us: fear and respect.

### THE FEAR FACTOR

When we live in fear of how an authority figure might respond to us if we do not obey, then we will usually follow their orders and instructions. But we will usually do so only for the purpose of avoiding the consequences that are sure to come our way if we do not comply. When fear is the motivating factor, our cooperation and compliance is based primarily on the notion that, "if I don't want to get hurt or suffer some other terrible and dreaded consequence at the hand of the one I fear, then I'd better do as they say."

## The respect factor

The second condition which may motivate us to cooperate and obey is respect. When we actually respect the authority figure in charge, then the fear factor is usually not necessary to gain compliance and cooperation. This is why it is important that we develop in our kids a respectful attitude toward us and other authority figures.

The fear factor shows up in our relationship with our kids well before any thought of respecting us is a consideration. Before they understand or are introduced to the importance of respecting us, they respond first to our authority out of fear. From the very first, "No," along with the look in our eyes that says we really mean it, it is fear rather than respect that provides the motivation for them to behave. They recall from past experiences what happened when they disobeyed, and they remember they did not like it!

It is at this early stage of our relationship with our kids—roughly between one and two years of age—that they fear us because we have the control, because they must obey and because they understand from past experiences that consequences are right around the corner if they do not. Respect is not yet present—it has not developed in them, and has therefore nothing to do with what motivates them as infants to cooperate and obey at this stage.

But all too soon kids grow older, and as they do it is essential that the original fear motivation be replaced with respect-based motivation. Unfortunately for far too many parents and their kids, this transition either comes too late or does not happen at all. As a result, they grow and develop into adolescents—and then into teenagers who either continue to behave and cooperate, but are motivated to do so based on the original fear factor that was not replaced by respect; or they cease to cooperate when they no longer fear their parents' authority.

Neither is a good or acceptable outcome. It is the task as parents then, (one of many!) to assist and support our kids in the transition from obeying and cooperating out of fear, to obeying and cooperating out of respect.

## IS RESPECT TAUGHT, OR IS IT CAUGHT?

The standard cry of many parents today is that what this world needs is more respect given and shown to adults from kids and teenagers. If kids showed more respect for their elders—and for each other for that matter—this would be a safer and healthier place for us all. If kids and teenagers had more respect for authority, there would be far less crime, violence, and destruction. If kids had more respect for parents, others, and the world they live in, life would be a far better experience for everyone!

As a parent, a therapist, and a resident of this far from perfect place we call Earth, I couldn't agree more with the notion that kids need to have a greater respect for their parents, each other, and for their world. Can you imagine the worldwide impact if kids were willing (knew how, would probably be more accurate) to have and show more respect? The affect would be like pushing the delete button on a computer: Selfishness—Zap! Aggressive behavior—Zap! Destructive attacks—Zap! Violence, crime, and wars—Zap! So much of what ails our crippled society would come to a screeching halt if only the younger generation would show more respect.

What I have difficulty with is not the notion that kids need to have more respect; this is a foregone conclusion. But many parents do not realize that teaching their kids how to respect others begins with they themselves showing respect to their children. In short, teaching kids how to respect others is a direct result of showing them the respect they need and deserve. If parents respect their kids, then the odds are good that they will grow up not only respecting their parents, but others as well.

As parents, it is easy for us to operate under the misconception that the right to be respected comes only with age and with time. In essence, many say to their kids, "Mind your P's and Q's for about eighteen years and then when you're an adult, I will show you the respect you have earned during that time." This is a common and often unspoken attitude that perhaps many of our parents had toward us when we were growing up. And now in our role as parents, we may be unknowingly passing this misconception on to our kids by way of our attitudes toward them.

Rights and privileges are in fact earned and certainly can be lost, but neither should be confused with respect. Our kids deserve all of the respect from us that we expect from them. Who of us has not heard, or perhaps ourselves said, "I'll teach you to respect your elders!" Yet, real respect is "caught" every bit as much as it is taught, maybe even more so; children "catch" respect by observing and experiencing how they are treated by their parents. I can assure you that kids who learn to respect their elders, others and authority figures, are almost always kids who have had respect shown to them.

## WHAT'S A PARENT TO DO?

There are many ways we send messages to our kids that we either respect them, or that we do not. Here are just a few:

Do you insist on using nicknames that your kids have clearly said they do not like or appreciate? My youngest daughter, Allyson went through a phase when she was young where she did not like being called "Ally." Her mom and I loved that nickname and loved having a daughter named Ally. Allyson, on the other hand, did not like being referred to in that way, and insisted (respectfully) on being called and referred to as Allyson. Reluctantly, but correctly, we began calling her by her full first name. She deserved our respecting her right to be called what she wanted to be called. Our insisting on calling her what we wanted because we thought it was cute would not have been giving her the respect she deserved. Her request was respected, not because she earned it, but rather, because it was her birthright. By the way, she reverted to wanting to be called Ally within a matter of weeks!

Do you disregard their feelings, thoughts or opinions? Kids should not have to wonder if they have the right to have certain feelings, thoughts, or emotions. Responses like the following may lead them to feeling they are not respected:

"Don't be silly (ridiculous, stupid, etc.). Of course your friends like you!" (End of discussion).

"Don't be so sensitive. I didn't mean anything when I said you're getting a little chubby. Lighten up!"

"Where in the world did you get such an idea? I can't even believe you said such a dumb thing."

Do you make jokes at your child's expense for the sake of a laugh? You may think you're laughing with them, but are they left feeling that instead, they are being laughed at, and once again, the butt of a joke?

Do you interrupt when your child is trying to talk, explain, or express themselves, and perhaps in ways that you would never tolerate from them? A good test question might be this: Would your best friend put up with your consistently interrupting them in the way you interrupt your kids?

What do you say to them about their friends? This is particularly difficult because sometimes you may not like a particular friend and will feel strongly that they are a bad influence. Certainly, a parent has not only the right, but the responsibility, to speak up but how you speak to them about their friends is just as important as what you say.

Do you treat your kids in ways that you want them to treat you? It doesn't mean an equal vote, it doesn't mean that you are not still the final word on decisions and it certainly does not mean that they have rights and privileges that cannot be taken away. It simply means that your kids have the same core worth and value that you have and this is best demonstrated by showing them the same respect you expect from them.

Do you ask your kids what they think or feel about a particular situation? It might be something from the news; it might be a fairly simple dilemma that you are facing at work or a decision you have to make: "Bradley, I've been trying to decide what to do regarding this particular problem. What would you do if you were in my situation?"

The goal is not to turn them into your therapist or life coach, nor to put undue pressure on them. And it is not even necessarily so important that you act on their suggestions. Sincerely asking for their opinions and ideas, and then genuinely considering them, will help you convey respect.

Do you regard their right to speak and be heard as every bit as important as your right? That's a particularly difficult one for most parents, because it is easy to confuse it with authority. The common misconception is that you might lose your authority if you let your children speak, and if you were to just listen. Actually, the opposite usually occurs. Your kids will be more likely to respect the position you hold as their parents if they truly feel heard. In the long run, agreeing with them or giving in is not nearly as important as being heard—really heard.

Do you let them know that you admire the way they handled a particular situation? It is easy to overlook the importance of compliments and speaking positively to children about their accomplishments. Knowing that they are actually admired by their parents is one of the loudest statements of respect. Don't hesitate to admire your kids, and remember the importance of going public with that felt admiration!

## WHAT'S THE BOTTOM LINE?

Respect is caught by kids more than it is directly taught. The need and right for respect is not based on age, nor is it earned by performance or ability. While rights and privileges are earned and can be lost, respecting your kids—just because they are your kids—is a constant, a right that must never be taken from them.

Respecting our kids, while not always easy or natural, is a fundamental necessity if we are to help them feel a sense of their own self-worth. If we are able to respect our kids just because of who they are, then they will grow up with a greater sense of who they are, and what they have to offer. They will also develop a greater capacity and desire to respect others as well. Raising great kids requires that parents show them they are respected just for being who they are. A good question that will help in assessing the respect you have for your kids is: do I treat my best friends and my kids in a similar manner when it comes to respect?

## DISCUSSION QUESTIONS:

1.  As a child growing up, were you respected by your parents?

2.  What signs of respect do you remember from them?

3.  What impact did their respect/non-respect have when you were growing up?

4.  Do you treat your best friend and your kids in a similar respectful manner?

5.  Do you agree or disagree with the idea that respect is caught more than it is simply taught to our kids?

6.  Are you succeeding at instilling in your kids a respect for others?

7.  What signs do you see that suggest that you are succeeding?

8.  In what ways do you show respect to your kids?

9.  In what ways do you see your kids showing respect (or disrespect) toward others?

*"If our efforts to motivate and influence our kids bring about desired behavior changes but at the same time create in them unhealthy patterns of being motivated by guilt, then we will have won the battle but unfortunately lost the war."*

# Question #3:

## *Do I use guilt to get my kids to do what I want?*

We've all heard the phrase, "winning the battle, but losing the war." Using guilt to shape our kids' attitudes and behaviors can lead to just that—our winning the immediate "battle," but eventually losing the "war." Guilt may work in motivating our kids in the short-term, but at the same time, it can create destructive life patterns in the long run. In spite of how destructive its use can be, it is difficult at times (especially when we have reached our limits and nothing seems to be working) for the best of parents to avoid giving into the temptation of using guilt as a last resort.

### Why it is tempting to use guilt on our kids

While there are many possible reasons that guilt so often becomes the go-to parenting tactic of choice, two stand out as the most common.

First, more often than not, guilt really does work (especially with very young kids) in getting our desired outcome. If immediate results were our only goal, then perhaps using guilt would be an acceptable way to go. But because there is much more to parenting than simply obtaining immediate results, inflicting guilt is not an option to be considered. Once again, we will likely end up winning the battle while losing the longer term war.

Secondly, for many of us, guilt was the change agent of choice used by OUR parents. If guilt were in fact a tool your parents used consistently throughout your childhood years, then it may be difficult (but certainly not impossible) to avoid a similar response with your own children. I suppose we could say that some of us parents come by using guilt naturally! (Chapter 5 will address in greater depth the issue of repeating the mistakes our parents made with us.)

Before giving in to the habit of using guilt as a motivational change agent, it might be helpful to consider what life patterns may develop in your kids as a result.

## WHAT TO EXPECT

1.  Guilt-ridden kids often grow up to be adults who have learned the fine art of manipulation. This is because they have learned to lie and manipulate in order to avoid the wrath of Mom and Dad's use of guilt. These kids often grow up to become parents who continue the pattern of using guilt to extract the desired change from their kids.

2.  Using guilt creates distance between parents and children. This provides one explanation as to why many kids and their parents end up estranged from one other. It also sheds light on how it is that so many parents lose the positive influence that is essential for them to have in the lives of their kids. It is

unlikely that any parent will be a positive influence on their kids when there is distance and separation between the two.

3.  When guilt is consistently used to get your kids to live up to your expectations, it may actually lead to more stubborn rebellion and defiance and as a result, your loss of necessary and appropriate control.

4.  The opposite may occur where under the load of feeling constantly guilty, they just give up altogether and become excessively passive and compliant. We have all seen kids who labor through childhood—and then well into their adult lives—with a broken spirit. They have given up, they avoid challenges and conflicts, and they refuse to try new things for fear of the guilt that might accompany failure. They develop a sense of false guilt and as a result, hold themselves accountable for just about everything that goes wrong around them.

5.  Guilt creates a tug-of-war effect rather than bringing parents and kids to the same side where they are more able to work together. Usually in a tug-of-war, it is either the strongest or most persistent who wins, not necessarily the one who is right. When it comes to tug-of-wars with your kids, no one ever really wins.

6.  Motivation by guilt creates an external motivational system rather than an internal one. Stated simply, kids who have been consistently motivated by guilt are often not guided by their own internal sense of right and wrong (conscience), but rather, by the need to avoid feeling guilty, along with the need to be accepted. The thought process then outside the home and among their peers may go something like this: "If my choice is

to either feel guilty and unaccepted because I act and behave differently than my friends, or to feel accepted and guilt-free because I conform, then I will choose guilt-free acceptance from my peers by conforming. I will do what it takes to get their acceptance and a freedom from feeling guilty."

7.  This pattern of being motivated by external peer expectations is likely to extend into adult life—being motivated by the expectations of others—rather than developing an internal sense of what is right and wrong. This can create a life-long pattern of blind compliance, the pursuit of acceptance, and avoiding feelings of guilt. Needless to say, there are significant dangers that arise when the expectations of others' becomes the road map for a child's behavior.

8.  Kids who have been motivated and shaped through the use of guilt at the hands of others are more likely to become parents themselves who are more easily manipulated by guilt—and sadly, often at the hands of their own kids. (The next chapter will discuss this in greater detail.)

## WHAT'S A PARENT TO DO?

Using guilt can be unintentional. For most good parents who want to be better parents, it usually is. Unfortunately, for others it might be overt and actually intended to hurt, control, even punish. But often the use of guilt is more subtle and not at all meant to be hurtful, controlling or destructive. Nonetheless, it can be.

Avoid responses like these:

"If you really loved your dad, you would help him more around the house."

"If you care about my sanity, you will give me a little peace and quiet."

"You make me look like such a terrible parent when you dress like that."

"Your constant back talk causes all sorts of pressures between your dad and me. Our marriage is hard enough as it is."

"It certainly doesn't seem to me that you could really care for your sister when you yell at her that way."

Compare the above messages, which combine a hint of motivation by guilt, with the following, more positive motivational messages. These messages are more likely to teach and instill a sense of responsibility rather than guilt:

"You are an important part of our family team and I expect more help from you than I have been getting lately."

"As much as I usually like being around you, right now I need a little space."

"I will not allow you to go out dressed like that."

"Your talking back is not acceptable. I want to hear how you feel and what your complaints are, but you must talk to me in a respectful manner."

"I know your sister can be frustrating at times, but you must learn to be more patient, and be a little more willing to put up with her."

## WHAT'S THE BOTTOM LINE?

Motivating and shaping our kids is certainly an important part of being a good parent—and a huge responsibility. Instilling a sense of right and wrong—feeling good when they do right and feeling badly when they do wrong—is also a big part of our task as parents. After all, isn't that what conscience development is all about? How we motivate our children plays a vital role in how they grow up viewing and valuing themselves and their world.

If our attempts to shape and to motivate them brings about immediate desired changes but create in them unhealthy patterns of guilt-motivated behaviors, then, truly, we will have lost the war. On the other hand, if we value and strive for not only appropriate behavior change in our kids, but the healthy and productive shaping of their character and conscience as well, then we must find constructive and growth producing ways of challenging them without employing the use of guilt. Since our goal is to raise great, healthy and anger-free kids, there is simply no place for the use of guilt in our parenting tool box.

## DISCUSSION QUESTIONS:

1.  Did your parents use guilt to get you to do what they wanted?

2.  If they did use guilt to motivate you, how were you affected as a child?

3.  Does the fact that that they used guilt (or not) have an affect now—on your life as an adult?

4.  Do you use guilt to get your kids to do what you want? If so, how does it seem to be affecting your relationship with them?

5.  How does your use of guilt seem to be affecting them in their relationships with others?

6.  If you consistently use guilt with your kids and want to change, what are some other ways you could motivate them?

*"Kids who are motivated and shaped by guilt are more likely to grow up and become parents who are more easily manipulated by their kids when they attempt to use guilt to get what they want."*

# Question #4:

*Do my own guilt feelings affect how I parent?*

IN THE PREVIOUS CHAPTER we addressed the temptation to use guilt as a means of motivating your kids to behave and to live up to your expectations. In this chapter, we are going to discuss how guilt-ridden parents are often more easily manipulated through guilt—and often at the hands of their own children.

## THE CONNECTION BETWEEN "GUILT-BY-PARENT" AND "GUILT-BY-KID"

When kids have grown-up being made to feel guilty when they fell short of parental expectations, the pattern of needing to please others in order to avoid the pain of guilt can eventually spill over into their relationship with their kids. Despite plenty of exceptions, it does often follow that children who have been consistently motivated and shaped through the use of "guilt-by-parent" are far more likely to be parents themselves who continue to be easily controlled and manipulated through "guilt-by-kids."

Look back for a moment, to your early childhood relationship with your parents, as well as to your early childhood peer relationships. Was the use of guilt to get you to behave in a certain way a common tactic used by your mom and dad? If so, did that pattern of conforming in order to avoid feeling guilty eventually become a pattern in your peer relationships? If so, is it possible that pattern may continue to influence how you parent today? Have your kids discovered that making you feel guilty works like a charm in getting whatever they want?

Since it is your goal to raise great kids who are free of inappropriate anger and self doubt, it's helpful to know and understand as much as you can about your own motivations and behaviors as a parent. Allowing your decisions as a parent to be swayed by your desire to avoid feelings of guilt is an unhealthy motivator that can interfere with your efforts to raise healthy kids. If your parents—and then your friends—used guilt to get you to shape up, behave, or manipulate you into being what they wanted you to be, then it's possible that this pattern will find its way into your relationship with your kids. The tell-tale signs of a continued pattern of motivation by guilt might be determined by watching for subtle attitudes, such as:

"If I can avoid feelings of guilt by giving in to my kids even though I know I shouldn't, then so be it." Translation: If we are more motivated by our need to please and to be accepted, than we are by our desire to be successful in raising healthy kids, then we are an easy target for "guilt-by-kids."

Thoughts of the guilt-motivated parent go something like this:

"If I were a better parent, Casey would love, accept, and listen to me more."

"If I really loved Brian the way I should, I would give in to his crying and give him what he wants."

"If I hadn't divorced Kelly's father, we'd have more money to enjoy life so I'd better do everything I can to make it up to her."

"I feel guilty that I have to work and be away from Ryan so much, so I will let him do what he wants to do when I am with him."

## SOME POSSIBLE RESULTS OF "GUILT-BY-KID"

All the above are just some of the thoughts and feelings of a guilt-ridden parent attempting to make their guilt go away. And yet, if we were to ask any parent who consistently gives in to the unreasonable and unacceptable demands of their kids, they would likely acknowledge that the more they give in, the greater and more unacceptable the demands become. Most would likely add that when they finally do say no—because they are out of time, patience, financial resources, or maybe just because they've had enough—their kids, who have learned to manipulate through guilt, really pull out all the stops in an effort to get what they want. It is at this point that Mom or Dad usually begins to feel even more guilt and less acceptance. A vicious cycle has been established, and one that is difficult (but not impossible) to break.

Another likely result of allowing kids to use guilt to get what they want is a spoiled child (eventually a spoiled adult) who has learned to capitalize on the guilt and insecurities of their parents. Such attitudes and behaviors can be very destructive in the lives of our kids as they grow up and develop other relationships. If your children succeed at getting their demands met because you so desperately want to avoid feeling guilty, then a pattern of thinking and behaving will develop that encourages them to make their "target" feel guilty until they give in. When they have finished with Mom and Dad, then they will understandably move on to friends, and sadly, to spouses. "It worked to get what I wanted with Mom and Dad," so the reasoning goes, "Why shouldn't it work with others?"

Kids who consistently and successfully use guilt on their

parents to get what they want may eventually grow up to be adults who have confused getting what they want with being loved. Needless to say, that's a dangerous and inaccurate assumption that can have disastrous results. When their effort to get what they want fails, they are left to conclude that they must not be loved. Hearing "no" sounds and feels like a personal rejection, rather than simply being denied. And of course, nothing could be further from the truth!

## WHAT'S A PARENT TO DO?

Absolutely nothing! Well not exactly. Let me rephrase that. There is nothing that can be done until you become aware of and understand that there is a problem. Only then will you be able to make some new and possibly tough choices.

If you are one of those parents who finds themselves giving in to their child's every whim in order to avoid feelings of guilt, take heart! By having read this chapter with an open mind and a willingness to look honestly at yourself, you've taken the first important step; you have increased your awareness of the problem. And now, armed with this new awareness, you will be much more able to effectively deal with the guilt in your life.

But along with this new found awareness comes the toughest part—trying out new and unfamiliar responses and making new and perhaps uncomfortable choices. New ways of responding to the demands of your kids may at first feel risky and you might even experience some frightening "catastrophic expectations" when you make new choices. After all, don't most new behaviors that have no guarantee of succeeding involve an element of fear? At first you may fear failure, possible loss, or rejection. You may even have to face your fear of being abandoned. In spite of your fears, I challenge and encourage you to call the bluff of your catastrophic expectations. And when you do, I suspect the end result will eventually be an improved relationship with your kids. And you will also help break a destructive pattern in their lives as well.

A little disclaimer: Being more aware of your motivations doesn't necessarily mean your days of feeling guilty will be immediately gone. In fact, you might even find that for a while, as you attempt to respond differently, that your kids will push back even harder. After all, using guilt has always brought their desired results, so they will not likely be willing to give up what has always worked so well and for so long!

It may also take some time and effort for you to break the cycle of feeling guilty when you say "no," to your kids. Feeling guilty when you do not please the other person is, after all, a lifelong, familiar pattern. But as you consistently work to create new patterns of behavior—even though at first your feelings may not immediately match your new behaviors—I assure you, over time you will eventually see your feelings, emotions and attitudes catch up with your new behaviors. Only then will your new efforts become more natural and maybe even effortless.

I suspect too, that eventually you will be relieved as you begin to see your kids responding positively to your refusal to be manipulated by guilt. I know, I know, easier said than done; but it will work and you will survive the process. Not only will your kids respond in a healthy fashion, but you will also make progress in weakening and perhaps eliminating altogether, a life-long pattern of destructive and self-defeating guilt. Please give it a try.

## What's the bottom line?

Understandably no parent wants to be motivated and manipulated by their feelings of guilt. However, when your kids realize just how strongly you want to avoid those feelings, you become easy prey and will be handily manipulated by them. Pleasing and constantly gratifying your kids for the sake of appeasing your guilty feelings does not a good parent make.

We cannot afford to be influenced by our own need to avoid feeling guilty. Being the parent our kids need does not always mean being the parent they want. We can't always be the good guy. That means sometimes saying no, sometimes not pleasing them, even though we may be left feeling guilty because we have deprived them. Naturally, this can bring about occasional and illogical feelings of guilt in the best of us, but we must avoid being shaped and driven by those feelings.

## DISCUSSION QUESTIONS:

1.  If your parents used guilt to motivate you when you were young, how did it affect your relationship with them?

2.  If they did use guilt in an effort to motivate you, did it work?

3.  In addition to affecting your relationship with them, in what other ways were you possibly shaped by their use of guilt?

4.  Do you ever find yourself, as a parent, being motivated by your own guilty feelings with your kids?

5.  If you do, what are some possible negative results of your being motivated by guilt in your parenting?

6.  If your kids are able to manipulate you through guilt, what are some possible consequences to their overall growth and emotional development?

*"In spite of our determination to avoid repeating the mistakes our parents made with us, we may still be influenced by them."*

# QUESTION #5:

## *Do I make some of the same mistakes with my kids that my parents made with me?*

WE'VE ALL HEARD IT BEFORE. We've all probably even said it ourselves: "Someday when I have kids of my own, I'm going to do things differently than my mom and dad did with me. No way am I going to make the same mistakes with my kids that they made with me!" But insist as we may, it is a challenge for most parents to escape the influence of their own parents. While changing bad habits in your parenting is not impossible, it usually takes a concerted effort to accomplish.

It is even likely that most of us have heard such a declaration from our own kids! Even if they weren't brave enough to actually say it directly, what parent hasn't occasionally seen that look in the eye of their kids that said something like, "Someday when I have kids of my own, I'm going to do things differently?"

I can recall a time or two (or more!) in my own parenting when I had to agree with my kids—that there might have been a better way of doing things. Just as we occasionally saw them evaluating and appraising our way of parenting them when they were young, I hope they will continue to think through some of the things we did as their parents, and not allow our mistakes to negatively influence how they decide to parent their kids.

The first step in correcting the mistakes our parents made with us is to look back. While not always the case, parenting patterns that were maintained by our parents when we were growing up our often the foundation of the struggles we may be having with our kids today. In spite of our determination to avoid repeating those mistakes, we may still be influenced by them!

Several examples might help to clarify just how we may, without knowing it, repeat some of the same mistakes our parents made:

Imagine for a moment that when you were a young child you had a little sister who tragically died in an accident. As a result, your parents became excessively overprotective of you, fearing the same fate could befall you. Understandably, the last thing they wanted was to lose another child. But in spite of their good intentions, their overprotective behavior left little room for you to explore, experiment, or to take important steps away from their constant protection.

Now as a parent, you have carried on the stifling pattern of being overprotective with your kids. There is no good reason for it, but you just can't seem to let go and allow them to experience a little freedom as they grow up and become more responsible. No current circumstances warrant your cautious style; it is just a parenting pattern to which you have become accustomed. Irrational fears dictate your actions rather than the current circumstances.

Now imagine that you grew up in a home where your parents were consistently harsh and critical of you and anything you tried to do. Nothing ever seemed to be good enough for them and they always had a "that's good, but" kind of attitude. In addition to their negative attitudes, they told you that the reason for their critical eye toward you was because they loved you and cared for you. As a result, you were left to conclude that (remember, kids have sponge-like brains that absorb whatever they are told or observe, as truth) the way to convey love is to be critical of the one you love. After all, isn't that what Mom and Dad said?

Eventually you marry and have kids of your own and apply the same critical response pattern. It is in this way that the parenting pattern—the mistakes made by your parents—gets passed on to the next generation. There is no real rationale or justification, but it continues to be a pattern that is passed on nonetheless.

Or perhaps your parents believed that respect from kids was important and that the way a child shows respect is by not questioning or speaking up with their thoughts or opinions. Furthermore, to ever complain about anything was viewed as a sign of disrespect and was therefore, never allowed under any circumstances.

Now, years later and as a parent, you believe in the importance of teaching your kids to respect others, a good and proper value indeed. (It might be helpful to review Chapter 1 for more on how kids learn the real value and attitude of respect.) Because of your parents' behavior and attitudes toward you and their efforts to teach you to be respectful, your expectation is that respect from your kids looks the same way—silent compliance. When questioned by your kids, even when done in a respectful manner, you conclude that they are being disrespectful. As a result, conflicts are unnecessarily created and then addressed inappropriately, based on the misconception that they are being disrespectful, rather than simply disagreeing with you.

These are just a few of the ways we may make the same mistakes as our parents. The examples could go on and on.

There is yet another way that our parenting efforts can be influenced by the mistakes of our parents. Rather than repeating their mistakes, we may actually do the very opposite of what they did with us. This too may have a negative affect on how we parent our kids, since the opposite of the wrong way of doing something is not necessarily the right way. All of this to say, in our effort to avoid repeating our parents' mistakes, we must be careful not to overreact in the opposite direction, since this too can be harmful. Again, a few examples may be helpful:

Suppose your parents were both deeply involved in their jobs and other activities. As a result they seldom spent quality time with you. Whenever you needed something from them, whether it was an activity you wanted them to be a part of, or maybe just a little time spent listening, you seldom felt that you were a priority to them. And when they did occasionally attend to you, it was reluctantly given and was rarely the kind of meaningful experience children long for. Basically you grew up feeling that you were a lot of trouble and that if your parents really cared for you, they would show it by giving more of their time toward having a relationship with you. You were usually on your own to play, entertain yourself, and to stay out of trouble.

As a result of your parents' neglect, you grew up concluding that when you became a parent you were not going to be like them; you would not make the same mistakes with your kids that they had made with you. You were going to be very involved in the lives of your kids. That's always a good thing, right?

But rather than giving and spending an appropriate amount of time and energy being involved and attentive to them, you dote on them and are always in the middle of whatever it is they are involved in. And without knowing it, you leave very little room for them to venture out on their own to develop as individuals. You become an over-indulgent, over-bearing parent who is willing to drop anything at any time in order to be involved in the lives of your kids—all for the purpose of giving them the time and attention that you never received from your Mom and Dad. (Refer to Chapter 8 for more on being appropriately available to your kids.) Certainly you have succeeded in not making the mistake your parents made with you, but the result of having done the opposite is likely to be either creating an unhealthy dependence on your presence and involvement, or resentment from your kids because you are always there. Most would agree that neither is an attractive option.

Imagine that as a child your parents were unreasonably strict and rigid. Not even the smallest infractions or misbehaviors got by them without some sort of consequence. And you swore that you would never conduct your home that way. A great decision so far . . .

But in your understandable desire to avoid your parents' error, you ignore many of the unacceptable behaviors in your kids—behaviors that should be challenged. In an attempt to avoid being excessively strict, you now provide few consequences, guidelines or expectations for your own kids. As a result they do not learn the necessary skill of cause and effect thinking which enables them to take into consideration the consequences for the choices they make. (For more ideas on establishing appropriate guidelines for your kids, refer to Chapter 20.)

When you were a little kid, your parents believed that if they helped you solve the problems that arose from time to time, you might become too dependent and reliant on them. So in order to avoid creating dependence in you, they offered little assistance, guidance or feedback. You were left to your own efforts to figure out the problems in life that came your way.

As a parent you are determined not to repeat that mistake with your kids. Once again, this is a great decision. But in that determination, you make the mistake of taking the opposite position of always being there with a solution anytime your kids have a problem. As a result, you prevent your children from developing good problem-solving skills and techniques. And the chances are very high that they will become adults with few of the problem-solving capabilities that are so essential to healthy and effective living.

## WHAT'S A PARENT TO DO?

Looking back in order to learn from the mistakes our parents made is the first step in assuring that history does not repeat itself. The next step in overcoming any unwanted behaviors and attitudes we may have inherited, is having the courage to try out some new parenting behaviors. At first, this may seem to be a hit and miss, trial and error approach—just as most efforts at new behaviors are—but your efforts will eventually lead to new and more effective ways of parenting.

Some wise person once said, "Who I am today, shame on my parents; if I stay this way, shame on me." While I don't endorse the notion of shame in this quote, I do agree strongly with the content of the message. We are not a "product" of the mistakes our parents made, but rather a product of how we decide to respond to those mistakes over the years. If we really believe this, then we have the incredible power and ability to overcome the mistakes others have made with us. On the other hand, if we choose to blame others, then we remain their victim, and we remain helpless. Both interfere with our ability to grow.

Fortunately, this applies to our kids and our efforts with them, just as it applies to the mistakes our parents made with us. Our kids do not have to be held captive by the mistakes we will inevitably make with them. They too, will have a choice to make as to whether or not they are going to be a victim of our mistakes, or whether they are going to grow beyond our errors. Hopefully they will make the choice to grow beyond the mistakes we will, without a doubt, make with them.

## What's the bottom line?

While it is not easy to do, it is important for all of us to look at and consider how our parents raised us. We must also be willing to evaluate what works in our relationship with our kids, and avoid what does not.

Simply stated, consider and evaluate the job your parents did with you. Then take the best and leave the rest. Take advantage of books, friends, professionals, as well as your own instincts, to create the most effective style of parenting for your kids. It can even be helpful to draw from how your parents raised you. But to either blindly apply, or to blindly reject their efforts will not serve you well in your quest to be a successful parent.

## DISCUSSION QUESTIONS:

1. How did the mistakes your parents made with you affect your relationship with them?

2. Do the mistakes they made when you were growing up affect you now?

3. Do you ever find yourself making some of the same mistakes with your kids that your parents made with you?

4. If you do, how do those mistakes you are repeating with your kids affect your relationship with them today?

5. Do you remain a victim of the mistakes your parents made, or do you feel you have let go and moved on?

6. Have you forgiven them for any mistakes they may have made as your parents?

7. If not, what do you think it would take for you to forgive them?

*"Raising kids who are self confident and free of chronic, self destructive anger requires that we start encouraging them from the beginning of their lives to have a sense of independence and self-reliance."*

# Question #6:

## *Do I encourage my kids to develop an independent spirit?*

THE TASKS AND RESPONSIBILITIES that come with being a parent are practically endless, but of all the many duties and responsibilities we assume as parents, none are more important than the task of shaping, influencing, and designing our kids to have a spirit of independence and self-reliance. From the moment they are born—well not quite, but very early on—it must be our goal to slowly but ever so surely work ourselves out of a job. While it is important that we not rush the process of weaning them from dependence upon us to independence from us, we must at the same time be vigilant in our efforts to work in that direction and to that end.

We humans are one of the few animals on the planet whose relationship with their offspring is intended to continue for a lifetime, well after we are needed by them for nurturing, sustenance, and protection. It is almost without exception that in the animal kingdom, shortly after the parents are finished with those tasks, the relationship between them comes to an end, leaving parents and offspring to go their separate ways. Simply stated, in most species, dependency is the primary glue that binds the relationship together; when the dependency ends, so too does the relationship.

Gratefully, we are unlike most other species in that we want our kids to love us (and to even need us in some ways) well beyond the years that their survival is dependent upon our care of them. It is our hope and prayer that as our kids move toward independence, that they will still love us and desire to have a life-long relationship with us. But if our relationship with them is to continue, it must eventually no longer be based on their dependence, as it does in most other species, but rather, on the fact that they value us in many other ways.

So encouraging our kids to be independent and to enjoy a spirit of self-sufficiency does not mean they will no longer need us in many other ways. After all, a significant basis for any relationship is the notion that we do in some way need the other person. As their parent, it is our job to make sure they develop independence so that once they no longer need us for their care and safety, their continued growth and survival will be in their hands rather than in ours.

It is true that initially the basis for our being loved by our kids is their dependence on us. After all, what information about us do they have to go on in those very early days, other than the fact that we are constantly caring for and attending to them? Of course they are going to love us during their early development and growth, but for little reason other than the fact that they depend on us and that we are there to take care of them.

Most of us would agree that being loved by our kids must eventually be based on far more than the fact that they are dependent on us. However, it is easy for some parents to fall into patterns that encourage their kids to remain dependent on them because they fear losing their love and affection. Rather than parenting in a way that broadens and strengthens their kids so they need them less and less, some parents may actually encourage reliance well beyond the point that it is necessary and reasonable. This pattern may be subtle and not consciously intended to discourage their independence since most parents really do want their kids to be self-reliant, and to develop the capacity of taking care of themselves.

## How our self-esteem affects raising independent kids

The problem arises when we confuse our being needed by our kids with our being loved by them. If you do not struggle with this yourself, you might be surprised at just how many parents do. When parents continue to relate their being loved with their being needed, they will understandably resist encouraging their kids to be more independent as they grow older. After all, if being loved by our kids were based on their remaining dependent on us, and helping them develop an independent spirit sets the stage for our no longer being loved, why would any of us be motivated to raise independent children?

It is often a sign of low self-esteem when parents believe that being needed and being loved are in some way related. If we struggle with our own sense of self-worth, then it is understandable that we might become motivated by our desire to be loved and to feel okay about ourselves rather than by the more important goal of raising independent kids.

The reasoning of some parents who discourage independence in their kids goes something like this: "If I want Jeremy to love me, then it is important that he remain dependent on me and need me. What other basis could he possibly have for loving me?"

The belief, either consciously or otherwise, is: "I'm not lovable or acceptable just the way I am. I must earn it by taking care of others. Now that I have kids, I can establish my self-worth by taking care of them and creating a dependence upon myself. Surely, if they need me, then they will always love me. If they don't need me, then I will be more 'leavable' than loveable to them." This reasoning is clearly a sign of low self-esteem.

The confusion between being needed and being loved does not always stem from the life-long presence of low self-esteem. In fact, it is possible to have had a good and healthy self-concept until a situation or event occurs that alters the otherwise healthy self-image. A common family life event that can damage a parent's self esteem may be an unsatisfying marriage, or even worse, a divorce.

When divorce or a poor marriage relationship occurs and a parent feels rejected and abandoned by their ex-spouse, it understandably may lead to a perception that they are more "leaveable" than lovable. This may then lead to a pattern of encouraging dependency in their kids. Since the "rejected" parent is no longer getting the love they want and need from their spouse, then the natural temptation can be to look to their kids to meet their need to be loved and to feel relevant. Their reasoning may go something like this: "If my kids need me, then they will have to love me and this will make up for the love I am not able to get in my marriage. Surely, someone out there loves (needs) me!"

Low self-esteem and poor marriages are just two of the unfortunate scenarios in life that can lead to discouraging the development of independence in kids by encouraging them to remain dependent. There certainly are other circumstances from which the pattern may develop but whatever the reasons, creating undue reliance on you as their parents rather than independence on themselves, can cause problems for them now and in their adult lives as well.

## Dependence and anger

Surprisingly, a common outcome that results when parents encourage inappropriate dependence is a child who actually grows up angry toward their parents for allowing and encouraging their dependence and reliance upon them. Sadly, the very effort to gain their love and acceptance, by fostering dependence, can turn out to have the opposite affect.

Dependent people are almost always also angry people as well. The anger that results from being consistently dependent on others may not always come out in the form of anger, but is nonetheless a common companion to dependence. It may come out in other ways such as passivity, impatience, irresponsibility, or some other hostile attitude like, "I'll show you world!" Since they have been robbed of self-reliance and independence—both basic human needs that affect the foundation of their self-esteem—they become angry. We have all heard the cry from a confused but perhaps well-meaning parent, "How can my kids be so angry with me after all I've done for them?"

An example of how encouraging dependence can lead to anger might be helpful:

Picture yourself sitting on a couch. Pretend also that every time you needed something, someone is right there to wait on you. Such a luxury might at first feel pretty good. After all, who wouldn't for at least awhile like to be waited on hand and foot, and relieved of the responsibility of having to do for themselves? I suppose that's why destination resorts are so popular—at least for a short period of time!

But consider what happens after an extended period of time of having been deprived of the responsibility of taking care of yourself. After weeks, months or perhaps years, you decide to get up off the couch and be more self-reliant. Into your first step, you now realize that you lack the muscle power needed to take care of yourself! You are physically weak, your muscles have atrophied, and you are now incapable of self-reliance. It is likely that the first person you will blame and be angry with is the one who encouraged you to depend on them instead of becoming self-sufficient.

An additional example—this one from the plant world— might help in describing the possible affects of inappropriate dependence in your kids. Quite a few years ago, there was a tall papyrus plant growing up into the overhanging limbs of a rubber tree in our back yard. Being the procrastinator that I am, I waited over a year or so before I got around to trimming the limbs of the rubber tree so the papyrus plant could grow freely without being supported by the limbs of the over hanging branches. All this time, the papyrus was relying on the strength and support of the rubber tree branches to keep it upright.

Having completed the task of cutting back the rubber tree that had for so long supported the papyrus plant, I was surprised when immediately the stems of the previously supported plant fell over. I soon realized that the failure of the papyrus stems to stand upright and independently when I removed their support, made perfect sense. While I am unable to explain this in biological terms, the simple explanation is obvious: for quite awhile, it was unnecessary for the papyrus to develop strength to stand on its own, relying instead on the support of the rubber tree. When its support was taken away and it was required to stand on its own, it was unable to do so.

When we consistently encourage dependence in our kids, they are more likely to grow up without the necessary skills, expertise and strength to perform the tasks from which we rescued them. Eventually, emotional and physical atrophy sets in and their "won't do it" ("because you will eventually do it for me") turns into a "can't do it." When that happens, they understandably become angry at the person who interfered with their developing a competence for living—you.

## WHAT'S A PARENT TO DO?

As in any other problem situation that may arise in our lives— whether it be physical, emotional, or relational—the more aware we are of what the problem is, the more capable we are of controlling how we are affected by it. Likewise, if we are unaware of the problem, it is more difficult to bring about the positive changes that are needed.

Stated simply, being aware gives us a greater degree of control over our circumstances. By having read this chapter, you have increased your awareness to any possible unwanted dependence which may exist in your relationship with your kids. As a result, you now have a far better chance of making the necessary changes.

Try to identify the reasons behind your creating dependence in your kids. Does your low self-esteem play a part? Are you attempting to get love from your kids that you are not receiving from your spouse? Are you confusing being loved with being needed? Ask significant people in your life to help keep you accountable in letting go of any unhealthy inter-dependence that might exist between you and your kids.

Do your best to take the necessary risks to break the cycle of dependence that may be interfering in your relationship with your kids. Begin to insist that your children do those tasks for themselves that you have typically done in order to keep their need for you alive. Remember that not only are you accustomed to the pattern of dependence, but that your children have also gotten used to your doing for them much of what they should be doing for themselves. Giving up their part of the pattern may be difficult for them as well.

Talk with them about any undesirable dependent tendencies that may have developed and let them know that you will be making some changes. Try to help them understand the importance of those changes and why they are necessary. Be as clear as possible and let them know what you will be expecting from them as a result of these changes. Remember that change of any kind is difficult and can even be frightening because the outcome is unknown.

Strive to avoid mistakes that are similar to the following:

When there is a school project that gets a little tough, you consistently come to their rescue by jumping in and doing it for them;

When you consistently take over their chores and complete them. You may jump in and take charge because they seldom do the quality work you expect. Or perhaps you just don't want them to have to work so hard;

When they are experiencing some relational problems, you consistently step in to solve the problem by telling them what you think they should do;

Taking over by choosing the classes you want them to take. Certainly you can have a say without making all the choices for them;

When it comes time to choose a college and they put off completing all those application forms, you protect them from failure by completing them and turning them in on time;

They have been told that the yard work has to be finished before going to the beach but you take over their task so they can enjoy the day with their friends.

Suffice it to say, when we create a pattern of dependence in our kids—regardless of our reason for doing so—we rob them of developing and establishing a level of competence that must be in place if they are to lead a competent, independent, and self-sufficient life of their own.

## What's the bottom line?

Raising confident kids who are free of chronic anger requires parenting skills that instill an appropriate sense of independence and self-reliance. From the very moment our children are able to walk, we must begin allowing and encouraging them to do for themselves. To do so does not mean that we are lazy, nor that we do not love them. It does not mean we are unavailable when our input is needed. In fact, it usually takes more time and energy to help, assist, and guide children than it does to simply do things for them.

The goal is not to raise kids who are so self-sufficient that they do not need others. Certainly having an appropriate need for others is the basis for healthy relationships, and it is true that "no man is an island." But it is essential to their health and well-being that they grow up to be adults who are capable of taking care of themselves.

If we consistently do for them what they should be able to do for themselves, the final outcome will be kids—and eventually adults—who are not only angry at us, but at the world as well, because they are unable to do for themselves.

## Discussion Questions:

1. When you were growing up did your parents encourage you to remain dependent upon them?

2. How did their attitudes regarding independence/dependence affect you as a kid? In what ways are you still affected?

3. Do you agree/disagree with the idea that parents must avoid allowing kids to remain dependent upon them?

4. How would you assess the issue of dependence/independence in your relationship with your kids?

5. If your kids are excessively dependent on you, what might possibly motivate you to encourage them to be?

6. Do you see any unwanted side effects developing as a result of their dependence?

7. If there is excessive or inappropriate dependence on you, what are some ways you could change the pattern?

*"While we must be diligent in protecting our kids, it is also important to recognize when our efforts to do so have gone beyond simply providing appropriate security, to an effort of creating guaranteed safety."*

# Question #7:

## *Do I excessively protect my kids?*

IN THE PREVIOUS CHAPTER ON DEPENDENCY, I suggested that a common motivating factor in parents who create and encourage dependency is their need to be loved. I also suggested that these parents have usually confused being loved by their kids with being needed by them. This misconception often stems from low self-esteem and the false assumption that the only way they could possibly be loved and accepted by their kids is if they design and create a relationship with them that encourages and is based upon dependency.

The underlying motivation of overprotective parents is usually somewhat different from this. While there may be similarities between parents who encourage dependence and those who overprotect, some may take an overprotective approach without necessarily needing their kids to be dependent upon them. Likewise, it is possible to encourage dependency without being particularly overprotective.

If overprotecting our kids is not usually motivated by low self-esteem and our need to be loved, then what is the reason? The most common and fundamental issue at work when parents are overprotective is fear.

This issue presents us parents with still another difficult judgment call—the task of distinguishing between responsible and safe parenting and the possible underlying need to protect beyond what is reasonable. Any effort to provide our children with complete and guaranteed safety would not be such a bad idea if only it were possible, but it is not.

## WHY SOME PARENTS OVERPROTECT

There are many possible reasons why you may have the urge to be overprotective with your kids. And usually, the motivations behind this pattern can be found by looking back at your own childhood experiences. Below are just a few of the childhood experiences that can set a parent up for becoming overprotective. If some of them seem extreme to you, I encourage you to plug in your own childhood experiences and consider how they may be influencing you to be overprotective.

As a child, you had a sister who was kidnapped. Now as a parent you have a difficult time letting your children out of your sight. Rather than teaching them the necessity of using caution, you overprotect them, making it unnecessary for them to learn proper caution for themselves. "If I fail to protect my kids," so the assumption goes, "then surely the same fate will befall my kids."

You were sexually abused by a soccer coach when you were young. Today you refuse to let your kids participate in any sport where involvement by a coach is necessary, unless you are present. Rather than teaching them what is proper and acceptable behavior by others, and what is not, you are ever-present to make sure they are not abused. "If it happened to me, then it could happen to my kids."

When you were young, you witnessed a friend get hit by a car. Today you are unwilling to allow your kids to walk anywhere without you. Rather than teaching them how to protect themselves by using proper caution, you provide the protection for them. "If it happened to my friend, it could happen to my kids."

You had overprotective parents who told you that their behavior was a sign of their love for you. As a result you have come to the conclusion that, "If I love my kids, I must protect and shield them from any and all harm, just as my mom and dad did for me." You have chosen to show your love by overprotecting them, rather than in normal and healthier ways.

When you were growing up you were the brunt of emotional attacks and jokes at school. Remembering how painful this social rejection was, you are now quick to protect your kids by rushing to school and demanding that something be done about the teasing your child is receiving from others. Rather than teaching your child how to deal more effectively with their difficult school situation, you take over, and in doing so, possibly provide more fodder for the jokes and abuse they receive at the hands of their peers.

Your parents erred in the direction of providing you with too little protection as a child. As a result you were left feeling unsafe and vulnerable. Now as a parent you conclude, "I will not make the same mistake with my kids that my parents made with me!" As a result, you over-correct your parents' mistakes by excessively protecting your kids.

## Some of the consequences of overprotective parenting

Overprotecting your kids as a result of your own fears and anxieties may prevent you from having a healthy and proper involvement in their lives. And when there is a consistent pattern of overprotective behaviors and attitudes, you run the risk of robbing them of some of life's richest experiences. In addition to interfering with life as it should be for them during their childhood years, overprotection may also create in them a sense of fear that will affect and limit them beyond childhood and into the rest of their lives.

Look back on Chapter 1 and what was suggested about the inability of young kids to question or challenge what they are told and what they observe or experience. During those early years of development, children tend to conclude and internalize whatever they observe and hear from their parents. Remember that this process can work in our favor as parents. But when there are persistent irrational fears on our part, it often works against us by creating similar irrational fears in our children.

When we protect our kids and provide safety for them beyond what is reasonable, we are likely to rob them of important experiences that might otherwise lead to growth, development, and maturity. If they are controlled and limited by our irrational fears while they are young and in our care, it is more likely that they will grow up to be adults who are unreasonably fearful. When this happens, we have done our children a real disservice.

Undermining confidence in their own judgment is another unwanted outcome of overprotecting our kids. After all, when we are overprotective, we send the message that they must trust us (and later on in life, others) rather than trusting themselves. Certainly there are times and circumstances when we want them to trust our judgment rather than their own, but our ultimate goal must always be to help them make the transition toward placing their trust in themselves to make safe, healthy, and responsible decisions.

## WHAT'S A PARENT TO DO?

Overprotective behavior can be subtle and far more difficult to detect than in the examples cited here. And providing a reasonable and appropriate degree of safety for our children is certainly a responsibility that should be taken seriously.

So how then do we go about determining the circumstances under which we should protect our kids and when we should rely on them to protect themselves? How can we know when our need to protect them is excessive and possibly based on fears from our own childhood experiences?

The following questions might help in the goal of maintaining a healthy balance between appropriate and necessary concern, and attempts to guarantee safety through overprotective behavior. While not always easy to answer, consider the following four questions. They should assist you in determining the differences between taking appropriate safety measures, and being an overprotective parent to your kids.

1.  At what point (and under what circumstances) have I done all that I can do to protect my kids?

2.  At what point must I trust the circumstances?

3.  At what point must I trust my kids to take the proper precautions that are necessary to protect themselves?

4.  When and under what circumstances can I let go and have the confidence that I have adequately instilled within my kids the good sense to behave in a way that now enables them to protect themselves as fully as possible?

## WHAT'S THE BOTTOM LINE?

All of our experiences and relationships during the course of our lifetime have influenced our outlook, our behaviors, and our attitudes—and ultimately, our role as parents. So it is natural for any parent who has had a traumatic experience to have the tendency toward being overprotective with their own kids.

It is also understandable that childhood patterns have a way of following us into our adult lives; if our parents were overprotective, it will be most natural for us to be the same. It is important, however, to remember that we can make new decisions in spite of our past experiences.

In order to avoid becoming an overprotective parent, it is essential that you understand your past experiences and relationships. Otherwise, you run the risk of robbing your children of the opportunity of living life to its fullest. As is so often the case, all of this is easier said than done, but it is nonetheless an important goal for parents to strive for. If it is our goal to raise healthy kids, we must not hold them back with irrational and displaced fears.

## Discussion Questions:

1. Were your parents overprotective with you as a child?

2. If they were, how did their overprotective behavior affect you as a child?

3. What affect might their overprotection be having on you today?

4. As a parent, are you overprotective with your kids, or do you provide them with appropriate and necessary safety?

5. How would the friends who know you best answer that question?

6. If you are an overprotective parent, what possible fears might lie behind your behavior?

7. If you are an overprotective parent, is unrealistic fear or a lack of self-confidence showing up in your kids?

*"Being physically present does not necessarily mean that we are available to our kids."*

# QUESTION #8:

## *Am I available to my kids?*

IT IS EASY TO CONFUSE being physically present with our kids and really being available to them. It is understandable too, that we might assume that if we are at home and "on the premises" that we have automatically made ourselves available to them. Certainly being physically present is important, and when we are, we increase the chances of our being available as well, but the two do not always go hand in hand.

A minister's wife once commented to me that although her husband's schedule allowed him to be around the house a good deal of the time, that she and her kids often felt like they were the only members of the church who did not have a "24 hour hotline" to him. Even though he was physically present much of the time, it seemed like just about everyone else took priority over his family. When a member of the church needed him, he would almost always drop what he was doing and attend to their needs. Her comments spoke volumes about the fact that being physically present does not necessarily equate to being available.

Ministers are not alone when it comes to the possibility of being present physically and yet unavailable. It is a pattern that the best of parents are in danger of falling in to. Next time you are on the freeway, just glance over at the car next to you. It won't take long before you see a parent consumed with whomever they are talking to on the phone, and little kid in the back seat all alone. In this day and age of iPhones, Blackberries, iPods, personal DVD players, busy schedules and of course, the law that requires young children to be in the back seat—children are too often ignored while parents do business, return calls, order dinner, or catch up with friends. Even though we are temporarily held captive together inside the same car, it has never been easier for us to be unavailable to our children.

Are you a parent who is able to be around more than most, and yet you are constantly distracted with volunteer work, tennis, or social clubs? Or perhaps you are constantly on the phone helping your friends?

Are you at home, but spending most of your time behind the sports page or logged on to the Internet?

Are you constantly in front of the T.V. and sending the message that you don't want to be disturbed?

Are you with your kids physically, but mentally checked out? If so, your presence does not translate into availability.

## ONE WAY OR THE OTHER, OUR KIDS WILL GET OUR ATTENTION

What does it take for our kids to get the attention from us that they need? For most of us—but for our kids especially—negative strokes are better than no strokes at all. This means that if they are unable to get the attention they need in positive ways and through healthy means, then they may do whatever it takes—even misbehaving—to get noticed. I believe that this issues alone helps explain why there is so much juvenile delinquency, gang violence, promiscuity and other social ills among teenagers today.

When we are willing and able to give our kids the kind and amount of positive attention they need, we will have a good shot at minimizing many of the negative behaviors brought on by their need for attention. When we do not give enough time and attentiveness to them it can lead to unacceptable behaviors that are, consciously or otherwise, designed to get our attention. After all, negative strokes (attention) are better than no strokes at all!

## But is it possible to be too available to our kids?

Once again, I can hear the skeptics, "Make up your mind. Are we supposed to be available to our kids or not!" Yes, but our being available to them does not mean that we drop everything anytime they demand our attention. In fact, it is possible to be too available, ready at the drop of a hat to attend to their every need. Some parents seem to be committed to the notion that nothing they are doing can ever possibly be more important than immediately shifting their attention and efforts toward meeting any and all of the demands of their children.

Not only can an excessively attentive style of parenting be harmful to your kids, it may also be detrimental to your own emotional and physical health and well being. Parents have needs that are important to foster and nurture as well. Most people who experience burn out in whatever it is they are involved in, do so because they have given too much for too long and simply get to the point where they cannot go on. Since we are into this parenting thing for the long-haul, it is important that we not only take good and appropriate care of our children, but ourselves as well.

Taking good care of yourself is also important to the process of modeling for your kids that they are no the only ones with needs. When you demonstrate to them that you have needs, they will be more likely to grow up understanding that others around them have needs as well. If we fail to model this, our kids are more likely to conclude that, since no one else seems to have needs that are as important as theirs then the world must owe them something anytime they demand it. In their minds they may become convinced that their needs are always more important than are the needs of others.

## Tantrums

It is safe to say that since the beginning of time there has never been a parent who has escaped the task of dealing with the issue of tantrums in their kids. Not only are tantrums inevitable in the parenting experience, it could also be said that they are to some degree and in some form even normal. It could be argued too that they occur for a good and understandable reason. After all, during the first nine months to a year of their lives, children have had their needs immediately attended to as they popped up, and for the most part, the world actually has revolved around them.

And that's the way it should be—at first. Understandably, it is a difficult transition required of them, to go from being the center of the universe (or as the behaviorist would say, having been raised thus far on a continuous reinforcement schedule), to being told "no." All of a sudden they are required to wait their turn, and are taught that others around them actually have needs too. Normal and inevitable tantrums are the fall-out of this rather shocking transition and it is important for parents to understand that they are a normal and inevitable occurrence in the process of raising healthy and well-adjusted children.

The difficulty with tantrums arises when a child is consistently successful in getting what they want. When throwing tantrums becomes a common and unacceptable behavior pattern, it is often a result of one of two behaviors on the part of the parent: Either we have continued to be consistently and excessively available and attentive to all their needs well beyond the year or so that it was necessary, or they have not received enough of the time and attention from us that continues to be necessary for them to thrive and develop. Both of these two extreme parental behaviors can lead to unacceptable and potentially destructive tantrums that are either a result of being addicted to excessive attention, or by having been deprived of adequate amounts of attention.

## TANTRUMS MOTIVATED BY ADDICTION TO ATTENTION

An excessively attentive parenting style often establishes an attitude of entitlement in kids and when expectations of immediate gratification become a way of life for them, they become addicted to the attention and compliance from others they have constantly demanded and received. When on occasion the expected and demanded responses from others are not forthcoming, they seem incapable of living without whatever it is they are demanding. Their addiction to attention and immediate gratification then, becomes a driving force in their lives. We all know people like this and most of us try to steer clear of them.

## TANTRUMS MOTIVATED BY HAVING BEEN DEPRIVED OF ATTENTION

It is ironic that our kids may develop the habit pattern of throwing a tantrum as either a result of having been given an excessive amount of attention, or of having consistently been given too little attention. When kids are consistently short-changed of time and attention from their parents, then the motivating factor behind their tantrums is the result of deprivation rather than addiction. They are like the starving person who, in their efforts to get the food they so desperately need, behaves irrationally and to the point of panic. Whether kids are motivated by addiction or by deprivation, the resulting tantrums are usually quite similar and always self-defeating.

## What's a parent to do?

Be willing to say "yes" to their need for our time and attention, but be willing to say "no" to them when it is appropriate as well. While there are no easy answers or recipes that guarantee a healthy balance of availability, asking your self this question may be helpful:

"Is what I am doing right now really more important than attending to and spending time with my kids?" Some parents will immediately assume that the correct answer should always be a resounding, "No. What I am doing can't possibly be more important." The over-zealous (and easily motivated by guilt) parent might actually think that to ever answer yes to this question would be selfish and irresponsible on their part. However, the truth is that there are times when what we are doing really is more important and maybe even more urgent. So based on the circumstances and the situation, saying no to your children will, at times, be the appropriate response.

How we communicate our response to their request for our time and attention is as important as knowing when to say yes, and when to say no. Regardless of our answer, it is important that we are aware of the tone of our voice, the look on our face, as well as the words we use. All three speak far louder and leave a more lasting impression than our actual answer to their request.

Do your tone, expression, and choice of words send the message that your children are a nuisance, a bother, and that you just wish they'd go away?

"Can't you see I'm busy?! Leave me alone so I can get this done!"

"Why is it that every time I get a chance to relax, you want something from me?!"

"If you hadn't kept me up so late last night, I wouldn't be so tired today."

"All right! All right! I'll be there in a minute!"

Few of us parents intend to send messages of this kind to our kids. And to do so once in awhile—followed by an apology—is not going to leave them scarred for life. Nonetheless, a consistent pattern of "go-away-and-stop-bothering-me" comments can shape the attitudes our kids have about themselves as well as how they see themselves fitting into our lives.

If you really do mean, "Not right now," then it is important to follow up with a rain check:

"I can't play checkers with you right now, but I would like to tomorrow night." The next night, be sure that you bring up the idea of playing.

"Give me just thirty minutes to unwind. Then we'll talk about what happened at school today." Once you have relaxed, be sure to initiate hearing about their day at school.

"I can't talk to you right now. Go on to bed and I will be in to spend some time with you in about ten minutes." When you have finished what you are doing, remember to follow through and spend the time you promised.

It is important to be present, in touch with, and actually tuned in to your kids. Without an attentive spirit and attitude (remember, your attitude is just as important as your attention), your kids will be less likely to be confident of their worth, their value, and what they have to offer. On the other hand, when they know that you value being with them and that they are not just an obligation, and when they know way down deep that you enjoy being involved in what's gone on in their day, they will be more likely to grow up liking and valuing who they are.

There is another benefit that is likely to come our way when we show our kids how much we value our time with them and make ourselves available to them—they will more likely grow up actually wanting to spend time with us when they are adults! When kids grow up with the confidence that they are more than an obligation, more than simply a responsibility, then chances are good that as they grow and mature, they will regard their parents as friends. This may be a peculiar notion to some parents, since the idea of actually being friends with their kids is not a common one. But it is possible, and it is one of the greatest gifts a successful parent can ever receive. And isn't that what most of us really want? Don't we really want our kids to grow up to be adults who want to be in a relationship with us?

At the risk of blowing my own horn, Joan and I succeeded at showing both our daughters that we enjoyed being with them, and that we valued being involved in their activities. They knew that they were far more than an obligation to us and that we valued their presence in our lives. They knew that going to dinner or to a movie with them when they were young was not an obligation, but a privilege that we looked forward to. Certainly there were many times that we did things with other adults where they were not included. But we always did our best to coordinate our activities in such a way that time with them was sacrificed as little as possible. As they grew into their teen years it was understandable that many of their activities became far more important to them than being with us, and that was alright. (OK, it hurt a little!)

Even though Ashley and Allyson grew older, and our time with them began to taper off some, they always knew how much we enjoyed and valued our time with them. Today, I am happy to say that we are very good friends with both of them. I can also say that they often go out of their way to do things with us and to spend time with us.

All of this to say that parents who invest time in their kids when they are small will not only help insure their success in raising healthy kids, but they will also increase the likelihood of enjoying a healthy and life-long relationship with them for years to come.

## What's the bottom line?

Being around our kids as much as is possible and appropriate is a great start toward our being available to them. But availability requires more than just physical presence. It takes our willingness to spend the time and energy to actually tune in to what's going on in their lives.

Shaping and influencing your kids—taking that "unfinished product" and "designing" them to become the healthiest person they can be—is every parent's responsibility. An important vehicle we have for accomplishing this task is your willingness to be available to them. If you are not around, you will miss the opportunity to influence them; if you are present but yet not really available because you are not tuned in to them, then you could still miss that opportunity.

While meeting their needs for time and attention is essential to their health and well-being, it is also possible to be excessively and inappropriately available to them. When parents are constantly available and believe that "no" should never be an option, they run the risk that their children will grow up believing the false assumption that: "Since no one else has needs that are as important as mine, then the world must owe me something anytime I demand it." Needless to say, such an assumption leads to many other problems.

## DISCUSSION QUESTIONS:

1. Were your parents appropriately available to you when you were young?

2. How did their degree of availability affect you as a kid growing up?

3. Is your availability to your kids today appropriate and balanced?

4. Do you ever wonder if you are too available to your kids, or do you need to work on being more available than you are?

5. Do you see any affects in your kids from your being either too available or not available enough?

6. If you believe you need to make some changes in this area of availability, what are they?

*"When we focus more on the positives in our kids, many of their negative behaviors may begin to fade".*

# QUESTION #9:

## *Do I focus more on my kids' positive or negative behaviors?*

IT IS NO SECRET that our kids do behave from time to time in ways that require us to challenge them (otherwise known as using corrective measures). The idea behind this question of whether we focus more on the negatives or the positives in our kids is in no way meant to minimize the value of challenging their unacceptable behaviors and attitudes.

In the introduction to this book, I suggested that, "we have all been given the honor, responsibility and privilege of taking a 'new product' that is far from perfect, far from complete, and applying our influences to create a healthy, responsible, productive human being." If we are to take this responsibility as parents seriously, then we must be willing, when necessary, to respond appropriately to the unacceptable behaviors and attitudes in our kids; those behaviors and attitudes that need shaping and influencing by us.

Most of us accept this responsibility of correcting our kids when it is necessary to do so. However, some parents make the error of ignoring and even disregarding all together the unacceptable behaviors and attitudes in their kids that should be addressed. Usually the mistaken assumption these parents make is that somehow age and maturity will eventually and automatically bring about the necessary changes and appropriate behaviors in their kids.

For others, focusing on negative behaviors and attitudes comes more naturally while acknowledging the positive in their kids is the more difficult task. This may be especially true if that was the approach your parents used when you were growing up. If our parents concentrated more on our negative behaviors than they did on our positive ones, then it is more likely that we will do the same in raising our kids. (Look back to Chapter 5 for details.) We could go on and on, blaming the previous generation for our parenting patterns, or we can break the cycle now with our kids.

The mistake of under-complimenting and over-criticizing may occur when a parent assumes that too many compliments might spoil their child, and that if they don't point out every behavior and attitude flaw they see in them, then those flaws will inevitably become a part of their character and personality. Nothing could be further from the truth. (What will spoil our kids is having too many "things" without the reasonable and necessary responsibilities and expectations to go along with those things. But then, that's another book!) Focusing on a child's positive efforts more than their negative ones does not create a spoiled child.

It is a false but widely held assumption that too much praise and positive recognition can encourage our kids to be satisfied and content. The fear and concern of some well-meaning parents is that when this happens, it will be the end of their child's motivation to continue improving and achieving. The reasoning seems to go something like this:

"If my kids are content and satisfied, then why should they continue to excel and improve any further? If I praise them too much, they will be content and satisfied with themselves and will be less likely to continue putting forth the effort to improve any further."

Satisfaction and contentment are quite different than passivity and complacency. When well-meaning parents hold this false belief, they tend to "economize" on their compliments and to withhold or limit words of praise, in the hopes that the absence of satisfaction will lead to greater motivation. They believe that while satisfaction and contentment is indeed the "carrot" to strive for, it must never be achieved. Otherwise, improvement may stop dead in its tracks.

## Consequences of excessively focusing on the negative

Although our motivations may be good, when we focus on the negatives in our kids in order to motivate them, our doing so may actually lead to the opposite results in them. This is due to the fact that as human beings, it is actually our experiencing contentment and satisfaction in a job well done that provides the needed motivation to continue improving and succeeding.

Focusing on their positive efforts does indeed lead to satisfaction and contentment but the results will not be de-motivation, but rather a desire to further improve and excel in order to keep the good feelings of success and contentment coming. This is because feelings of contentment and satisfaction are usually going to be rather short-lived in kids—in adults too, for that matter—if their successes are not continued. I like to think of it as satisfaction and contentment having a "short shelf-life." So for this reason, it is not likely that our kids will rest on their laurels because they are satisfied or content. Instead, they will likely be motivated to accomplish even more for the continued reward and benefit of feeling satisfied and content in a (continued) job well done.

When we consistently maintain an "economy on praise" with our kids, a number of unfortunate outcomes are likely: either they become driven perfectionists who are seldom if ever satisfied or pleased with their own efforts, or they become what I refer to as a "fallen perfectionist."

## THE PERFECTIONIST

In this scenario, the over-criticized and under-complimented child eventually takes over where their parents left off. In place of criticism from others, they become self-critical, judgmental and hard pressed to see any success in their own efforts. Since others have been reluctant to praise and compliment a job well done, they find it next to impossible to praise any of their own attempts that are short of perfect. This attitude of self-criticism often continues into their adult lives where they demand perfection of themselves and of course, never achieve it. It may also show up in their relationships, where they refuse to be satisfied by the efforts of others. For the perfectionist, every day is another day of inevitable failure since seldom do they achieve perfection.

## THE FALLEN PERFECTIONIST

The second scenario that may result from our focusing excessively on the negatives in our kids is what I refer to as a fallen perfectionist. This is someone who consistently sets goals for themselves that are significantly below what their actual abilities are. By expecting very little—or even nothing—from themselves, they avoid the pain, sense of failure and frustration that they have previously lived with because their successes have not been acknowledged and their best has seldom been accepted as good enough. The fallen perfectionist simply stops caring, and in turn, stops trying. They may fail, but it is OK. Skid Row is full of fallen perfectionists, but they can be found in many other life settings as well.

Neither a perfectionist nor a fallen perfectionist is a description of our kids that any of us parents set out to intentionally design. However, we may inadvertently do so if we do not allow them to experience contentment and satisfaction throughout the course of their young lives.

## WHAT'S A PARENT TO DO?

As is so often the case in this parenting journey, the appropriate balance between two extremes is a fine line we must find and then walk. Being an effective parent calls for finding the balance between ignoring what negatives can be ignored, and addressing those behaviors and attitudes that are serious enough to merit response and correction.

Likewise, we must load on the praise and the encouragement where it is appropriate. At the same time it is important to teach our kids that internal rewards for their efforts are also important, and that there will be times when praise from others is not forthcoming. Learning to live without constant external praise will help them avoid the danger of being addicted to the recognition of others. When we find and apply the proper balance we give our kids permission to feel truly satisfied and content with themselves and the efforts they make regardless of any acknowledgment they might receive from others. Stated simply, our goal is to help mold and shape their belief in the idea that acknowledgment from others for their accomplishments is icing on the cake rather than the cake itself.

A simple rule of thumb is to limit our corrective comments to the issues that really matter. Once again, it is easier said than done since we can't always clearly know which ones matter and are important to address, and which ones are not. Even though it is sometimes difficult to know the difference, it is important to consider.

There are some behaviors that are just marginally unacceptable and may be nothing but an isolated incident that will not be repeated even though we decide to ignore it. It is wise to take the position on minor issues that if it happens again, we will deal with it then. However, if it does happen again, it is important that we do.

If I ignore what just happened, do I run the risk of encouraging a full-blown and unacceptable behavior pattern to develop? Often the answer is that we could run that risk and so we respond with a challenge in order to avoid a probable bigger problem later on. At other times however, we will find that ignoring the small divergence from what's acceptable does not lead to further and more difficult problems.

Sometimes a simple response like, "You're better than that" to something that needs to be corrected sends both the message of our displeasure, as well as an appropriate positive expectation for them to live up to. Like most decisions we will face as parents, whether to respond or not (as well as how we should respond when we do) is a difficult one to determine. But when we evaluate in this way before responding, we avoid the risk of reacting to any and every little thing that comes along. Once again, we are challenged to decide, and we won't always get it right. It might be good to be reminded here that our kids really don't need perfect parents, but they do need parents who try their best to get it right.

Avoid, "That's good but . . ." comments. We may think we are complimenting and giving encouragement, but what we are really doing is sugar coating our criticism. When it is necessary to criticize or challenge them, do it in an open and honest fashion and in a way that does not destroy or damage their spirit. Breaking their will—their desire to do whatever they want whenever they want regardless of the circumstances to themselves or to others—is one thing; breaking their spirit—their enthusiasm, energy and excitement for living life—is yet another.

Remember that different responses may be called for depending on whether what just happened was an honest mistake by a little kid who is just learning how to live, or if what happened was a little kid challenging your authority. Most behaviors could potentially be either a mistake on their part, or it could be an attempt to challenge your authority. How to respond will be determined largely by how you answer the question: "Did Amy just make a mistake, or did she challenge my authority?"

It is not always an easy task to decide, before you respond, whether your child just made a mistake or if they were attempting to usurp your authority. It is difficult because very often, the only difference between the two is the motivation behind their behavior, so we must do our best to determine just what that motivation is before we can decide how to respond.

I am reminded of an incident that happened when our oldest daughter, Ashley, was three years old. We were guests at a friend's home, had just finished dinner and were about to start in on a dish of ice cream that had been served for dessert. There was a bowl of chocolate syrup in the middle of the table for us to help ourselves to. The three-year-old son of our host was sitting next to our daughter and as the syrup was passed he took a portion for himself and then proceeded to put some on her ice cream. I suppose he just figured that if he liked chocolate on his ice cream why wouldn't Ashley? I think too, that he was also just trying to be a good host to her.

Although it was too late, she kindly said that she didn't want any chocolate on her ice cream. Immediately the young boy's father (who, by the way, was a very good parent) slapped his son's hand and criticized him for putting the chocolate sauce on Ashley's dessert. He had mildly punished his son for what was clearly a childhood mistake that called for instruction rather than a punitive approach. Our little host had simply not yet learned in his three short years of life, that it would have been better to ask his guest if she wanted chocolate syrup on her ice cream.

A bewildered look came over his face as if to say, "I don't get it!" Then within a second, the look of surprise and confusion was replaced with a look of defiance that seemed to say, "I'll show you!" He then reached over and slapped his dad back, as if to even the score. To my surprise, he ignored his son's defiant slap and paid no attention to the fact that his authority had been challenged. In ten short seconds, our host had punished his son for a childhood mistake, and ignored his act of defiance.

Certainly this is a small and rather insignificant event. And every good parent has made the same or similar error of confusing childhood mistakes with attempts to overthrow their authority. However, it does serve as an example of how easy it is to confuse the two possible motivations behind such behavior.

It is easy to forget that our kids—being the, "new product" they are—can be clumsy, slow, careless, awkward, and ill-equipped for many of the social circumstances in which they find themselves. Younger kids especially have not yet had enough life experience to help them develop the social and physical skills they need in life. When we take the time to distinguish between their many childhood mistakes and their attempts to challenge our authority *before* we act, we help provide them with the experiences necessary to develop those skills.

## WHAT'S THE BOTTOM LINE?

We do our kids a great disservice when we neglect our responsibility of giving them feedback that challenges them to grow and to improve. If it is our goal to raise healthy and balanced kids, then giving guidance by way of well placed and well worded corrective feedback is an important part of the task and responsibility of accomplishing this goal. Everyone can grow and improve from being challenged and our kids are no exception.

They will also grow and prosper emotionally in response to their consistently hearing positive reinforcement from their parents—even when they may not have accomplished what they set out to do. When we tell them on a regular basis how well we think they are doing and how much we believe in them, we help them discover and to develop what it is they have to offer. And when we focus more on their positive behaviors and less on any of the negatives that could be ignored, we may even see some of their negative behaviors fade without our having to address them.

Satisfaction and contentment in a job well done do not lead to a decreased level of motivation in our kids. In fact both actually provide much of the motivation necessary for continuing to do their best. This is because both feelings of contentment and satisfaction tend to have a "short shelf-life" and in order to maintain them both, continued effort and success is necessary.

When we stress the negative in our kids, we run the risk of breaking their spirit by undermining their enthusiasm, energy and excitement for life. Without intending to do so, dwelling on and emphasizing their negative qualities rather than their positive qualities, can lead to a pattern of perfectionist tendencies that will interfere with their ever feeling a sense of success or accomplishment. Alternately, undue criticism may instead lead to what I refer to as a fallen perfectionist pattern of behaving. When this occurs they may lower their own expectations and goals in order to avoid feeling guilty for failing.

## Discussion Questions:

1. When you were growing up did your parents focus more on your positive or negative behaviors and efforts?

2. How did their positive (or negative) focus and feedback affect you and your desire to achieve?

3. As a parent today, do you focus more on the negative behaviors of your kids, or does your feedback emphasize their positive qualities?

4. Do you see your feedback having an effect on their ability to be content and satisfied?

5. Do you ever see signs of perfectionism that may be robbing your kids of feeling contentment and satisfaction?

6. Do you ever see possible signs of a "fallen perfectionist" in your kids?

7. What possible influence might you have on your kids and their desire to achieve and improve, as well as their ability to experience satisfaction?

*"Holding a grudge when our kids have disappointed us sends the message that our love and acceptance are both conditional, and that they must somehow earn back the privilege of being loved again by us."*

# Question #10:

## *Do I hold grudges?*

NOT ALL OF US fall into the behavior pattern of holding a grudge when our kids have disappointed, hurt or angered us. Nor do all of us resort to this sort of destructive pattern when our authority has been challenged. You may very well be a parent who does not resort to holding grudges against your kids, and if it does happen, it is done unconsciously. However, I encourage you to keep an open mind, and to continue reading before you write yourself a complete bill of health on this one.

How easily do you forgive? If your kids must say they are sorry before you are willing to forgive them, then you may be holding a grudge.

When they do say they are sorry, do your behaviors and attitudes suggest that you are waiting for more from them before your relationship can be back on track? If so, you may be holding a grudge.

When your kids hurt you, what does it take from them, before you are willing to reconcile? If they must go through a check list of requirements before you forgive, then you may be holding a grudge.

Do you build a barrier of silence and withdrawal when they have let you down, disobeyed, or failed to live up to your standards? If so, you are holding a grudge.

How you answer these questions will provide some insight as to whether or not holding a grudge plays a role in your relationship with your kids.

## WHAT MAY MOTIVATE US TO HOLD A GRUDGE?

There are a number of reasons why parents may resort to holding grudges against their kids. Four stand out as the most common:

1. Control
2. Pride
3. Punishment
4. Self-protection

## CONTROL

The fine art of holding grudges is a technique we humans use (consciously or otherwise) to gain and maintain a degree of control over the person whom we feel has wronged or disappointed us. A common perception, that often comes with having been hurt or disappointed by someone, is that by their actions, they have somehow gained a control over us, if only for a moment. In an effort to regain that control, we may resort to holding a grudge toward them.

## PRIDE

"One-up-man-ship" (Now it's MY turn!) may often be a motivation for holding a grudge. We may somehow feel beaten and defeated by the other person and what they've done, and as a result—ashamed or embarrassed. In order to save face, we hold a grudge to regain our pride.

When we hold a grudge it may be a way of insisting that the person who hurt us earn back a place in our lives by demanding that they demonstrate to us just how much they like, care, love, or value us. Without this evidence of how they feel toward us, our pride will not let them back in to our lives.

## PUNISHMENT

Holding grudges with our kids can also be a way of indirectly punishing them. Needless to say this is never an acceptable disciplinary response on our part. Talk about winning the battle and losing the war! There is no better example of doing just that, than using grudges as a form of punishment. Your kids love you deeply, and need that love returned. When you hold a grudge as a form of punishment, in their mind it calls into question your love for them. They so desperately want and need your love that they are usually (at least during those early years of development) willing to do anything to remove the grudge and to restore love. But this doesn't work for long, and it is a poor motivator for bringing about change and will inevitably and eventually backfire in relationships—especially with children.

## SELF-PROTECTION

Of the four most common motivating factors, self-protection may be the most common. Maintaining a grudge may be an attempt on our part to protect ourselves from being hurt again. As long as we maintain a grudge, we feel safe. It serves as an invisible but protective shield and in our minds, establishes the justification for maintaining a distance.

Grudges are a futile way of demanding a guarantee that "it" won't happen again. When it happens with our kids it is a way of protecting ourselves from being disappointed, let down, or in some way crossed by them. The message can be sent in a variety of ways, but the fundamental content of the message is always: "Prove to me that I can trust you, and until you do, I will maintain my grudge in order to protect myself." And yet if proof were possible, then trust in relationships would not be necessary.

Although it is never justified, it is especially tempting to hold a grudge against our kids when we think they have made us look like a bad parent ("look how you've made me look!") by calling into question our effectiveness as their parent. It is unreasonable for us to expect our kids to make us look successful (or to make us look any way, for that matter). It isn't their responsibility to make us look good, qualified, successful, emotionally healthy, or together in our role as their parent. And yet, most of us from time to time expect just that from our kids—to make us look good to the neighbors, their coach, the teacher, our parents, God, or to the church. Maybe we just want them to make us look good to ourselves.

As I am writing my thoughts on the subject of holding grudges with our kids, I am painfully reminded of an incident that happened between my youngest daughter, Allyson and me. Sad to say, but as I recall the incident, it occurs to me that just about all four of the basic motivating factors behind holding a grudge (control, pride, punishment and self-protection) can be found in this one recollection of mine!

Allyson was five at the time. I was supposed to pick her up from school, but on this particular day, I was running late. I was anxious about it because I knew that the school wanted parents to be prompt at the end of the day. When I got to the school, there was Allyson, waiting along with her teacher. Both were tolerant of my late arrival and it was really not a big deal. But rather than taking responsibility for my tardiness and apologizing, I looked down at Allyson and asked her to say "thank you" to her teacher for waiting with her. That was probably not an unreasonable request, and even though I was the one responsible for her teacher having to wait, a simple thank you would have been appropriate (an apology from me was also in order but the teacher didn't get that either).

Allyson, who was typically cooperative and responsive to our efforts to teach good manners, was apparently not in the mood to live up to my expectations of her that day. I asked firmly at least three times for her to say thank you to her teacher, and each time my requests were met with the same icy silence. Each time, too, I became increasingly embarrassed because Allyson would not perform for me (I have often wondered if she knew at the time that I was the problem, and that the circumstance really called for an apology from me more than it did a thank you from her). In any event, as we left, I remember holding a grudge. I remember feeling that she had let me down, made me look bad, and had failed to show her teacher what a great parent I was.

All the way home, I held a grudge through silence (after a few harsh words, that is). She knew that I was angry and disappointed. If the truth were known, she probably knew that I was angry and disappointed with her for no good reason but nonetheless, she was hurt and sad because our close bond—that was so familiar and pleasing—was, at least for the moment, broken by my grudge.

The story does have a happy ending. Fortunately, I realized fairly quickly how foolish I had acted, and that the problem was me, not Allyson. I knew that I was holding a grudge for the purposes of punishing her, and I could clearly see what that grudge was costing both of us. I hated the feelings that I was causing because they were so contrary to the closeness that was typical between the two of us. Before bedtime that night, I was able to go to Allyson and tell her that I was sorry, that I loved her and that I didn't want my mistake to come between the two of us. We were once again in a healthy place with each other and it felt great. And

I was reminded that it is not only OK to apologize and to ask forgiveness, but that it is essential to good parenting. (For more on the importance of being able to apologize, see Chapter 11.)

## WHAT TO EXPECT WHEN WE HOLD GRUDGES

Not only will holding a grudge create distance between you and your kids, but it also fails to guarantee that whatever it is they have done won't happen again. A common form of holding a grudge is to withdraw physically and emotionally, subtly demanding that they assure "it" will never happen again. But it will happen again.

Consistently holding grudges sends a message, that your love and acceptance are conditional, and that your kids must somehow earn back the right and privilege of receiving your love again. Kids who grow up and become healthy adults are not usually burdened with the threat of losing the love of their parents, not even temporarily.

Although it is important to avoid holding grudges against our kids, it does not require that we never be angry, disappointed or hurt by them. We will no doubt be all of those and more during the course of raising our kids. When we hold a grudge after being let down, we send a message that not only undermines their self-esteem but damages the quality of our relationship with them as well.

## WHAT'S A PARENT TO DO?

Once again, the first step toward overcoming any unhealthy parenting pattern is to recognize and acknowledge it. When we are unaware that there is a problem, we will be unlikely to ever overcome it.

When we want to eliminate an undesirable behavior in ourselves—in this case holding grudges—it is helpful to not just put our energies toward getting rid of the behavior we dislike, but to actually put an effort into replacing it with a new and more productive way of behaving. Here is one example of replacing an undesirable behavior—a grudge—with the more acceptable and desirable behavior of communicating a direct message:

When your kids are acting or behaving inappropriately, rather than holding a grudge, express in a calm fashion, that you are hurt, mad, angry, (or whatever you are). Let them then know that you expect something different from them, that you still of course love them, but that you expect changes in their unacceptable behavior/attitude. Finish by stating that there will be consequences, and what those consequences are, should they choose not to cooperate. This kind of communication accomplishes far more and leaves no battle scars; while holding grudges accomplishes nothing but to create a distance between you and them.

Also keep in mind that there may be times when you find yourself holding a grudge against your kids even though they really haven't done anything unacceptable or wrong at all (refer to my real life experience with Allyson). Avoid at all costs holding a grudge against them because they are unwilling or even unable to make you look good, or to help you feel better about yourself. It isn't their responsibility to do so.

## What's the bottom line?

When we hold a grudge it is often a sign that we have not yet forgiven our kids when they have disobeyed or disappointed us in some way. And when we resort to holding grudges rather than expressing forgiveness, it is usually an effort on our part to do one or all of the following:

- To regain the control we may believe we've lost;
- To heal our pride that has been hurt by the actions of our kids;
- To teach our kids a lesson by punishing them.

Whatever your motivation might be, holding a grudge is never an acceptable response to your kids and the consequences are sure to interfere with the kind of parent you want to be, as well as the parent your kids need you to be for them.

## DISCUSSION QUESTIONS:

1.  When you were growing up and you misbehaved or disappointed your parents, did they ever seem to hold a grudge against you?

2.  If they did, do you remember how their responses affected you?

3.  Do you ever find yourself holding a grudge with your kids for disappointing, misbehaving or letting you down in some way?

4.  If you ever do hold a grudge with your kids, how do they seem to be affected?

5.  If you do hold grudges with your kids, what do you understand about why you might do this (self-protection, revenge, modeling after your own mom and dad, etc.)?

6.  If holding grudges is a pattern in your responses to your kids, what affect does it have on your relationship?

7.  Can you see any alternative behaviors and attitudes on your part that might be more helpful and less damaging to your relationship?

*"Our kids are shaped and affected more by how we respond after we make a mistake, than they are by the actual mistakes we make."*

# Question #11:

## *Am I able to say, "I'm sorry. Will you forgive me?"*

HAVE YOU EVER NOTICED THAT when you ask your kids to apologize for something they've done or said that usually the most they are willing to do is to mumble a weak, barely audible, "Sorry." And while they may be able to pull off the minimum requirement, more often than not they'll do their best to avoid using the personal pronoun, 'I.' Come to think of it, many of us adults seem to do the same thing when we find ourselves in a situation where we need to apologize!

### WHY ADMITTING WE'RE WRONG AND SAYING WE'RE SORRY IS SO DIFFICULT

Our resistance to admitting we are wrong is due in large part to the natural human instinct we all have to protect ourselves. While there are no doubt others, there are three primary factors that usually influence our need to protect.

## PRIDE

As challenging as it is for most of us parents to apologize to our kids, it is even more challenging to include a request for forgiveness. This is because it takes an even greater dose of humility and absence of pride is necessary to ask for forgiveness. This is because when we move beyond just saying we are sorry, and risk asking for forgiveness, we have no guarantee of how they will respond. What if they say no?

We may hear:

"Maybe."
"I don't know."
"Beg a little."
"You'll have to earn it and I'm not going to make it easy."

Being faced with all of these dreaded possible responses from our kids requires that we set our pride aside before we are able to take the necessary risk of being hurt or possibly manipulated by them; all for the sake of reconciling with them.

Looking back on the time I held a grudge against my daughter, Allyson, I recall clearly wrestling with my pride: What if she says no? What if she uses my admitted error against me? Could my confession and request for her forgiveness undermine my influence in her life? It was this wrestling match that caused me to wait five hours before finally going to her to acknowledge my error and to ask if she could forgive me.

As I recall, I had decided early on that I needed to apologize. But it was the prospect of actually asking her if she would forgive me that was the toughest part of my task. By confessing and then asking forgiveness, I had to set my pride aside and be vulnerable to rejection, even humiliation. The only acceptable answer my vulnerable ego cared to hear was, "Yes Daddy, I will forgive you." By the way, I am glad to report that this response was what she offered and our relationship was again on track.

We all know that we are imperfect and few of us parents would deny this. But for many of us, it is yet another thing to set our pride aside and to allow our kids to see our imperfections first-hand. To actually say, "I'm sorry," is a risk of humility that many of us are not even willing to take in our friendships with other adults. How much more difficult it is for us to allow our kids to see our flaws and imperfections!

## Competition

It is easy for us parents to fall into a kind of competitive relationship with our kids. When this happens, we set a tone of "win/lose." While we run the same danger of this happening in our relationships with others, it is even more destructive when this competitive, win/lose pattern occurs between family members; when one person in an intimate relationship wins and as a result the other loses, then both have lost.

Just one of the many consequences of falling into a competitive relationship with our kids is that when we do, both of us may be more reluctant to expose flaws and short comings. In the business world, it is considered foolish and counter productive to share with the competitor ones weaknesses and vulnerabilities. The thought being if one acknowledges weaknesses to the competition, the information will be used against them.

This all makes sense in the competitive, "survival of the fittest" business world. But when the relationship with our kids takes on a similar competitive, win/lose tone, then the risk of being vulnerable enough to say we are sorry (when we really are) and asking forgiveness (when it is necessary) becomes very difficult to do.

## FEAR

It is a misconception of many parents that apologizing to our kids, will jeopardize their respect for us. It is natural to fear that if our kids were to see our weaknesses, imperfections and vulnerabilities, then they might no longer be willing to look up to us, obey us, or allow us to be an authority in their lives any longer. Being an influence to them is necessary and desired, and the possibility of losing that role in their lives is simply not something any of us wants.

But this is an unfounded fear—since nothing could be further from the truth. And the irony of this false assumption is that most of us actually look up to and admire those people who are willing to be vulnerable and to acknowledge their flaws—people who are willing to ask forgiveness when it is necessary. I believe it works the same way in our relationship with our kids.

## WHAT ARE THE BENEFITS TO ASKING FORGIVENESS WHEN IT IS NECESSARY?

Although we may fear losing control, influence and respect, when we are able to say we are sorry and then ask forgiveness, we are actually more likely to gain the respect and authority that we want. Perhaps if they were to see repeatedly that our apology is not followed by an effort to improve, or if they sense a lack of sincerity from us, we may then lose their respect. But when they believe we are sincere and they see us accepting apologies from them when they ask (see that we don't hold a grudge), then we will develop a foundation that will foster the growth of respect. And grow it will!

In addition to increasing the respect they have for us, there is another benefit to be gained when we are willing to ask forgiveness. When our kids see humility and honesty in us, they will be more likely to trust us. And because of their increased trust, a result of our willingness to risk by being vulnerable with them, then it is likely that they will show a similar openness with us.

Increased trust and a greater willingness to take risks means more dialogue, more seeking us out for our opinions, and ultimately, even more trust. Since taking risks is an important foundational ingredient in the growth and development of any relationship, then it stands to reason that the parent-child relationship is bound to grow.

## What's a parent to do?

Our kids will remember and be far more affected by how we respond after we make mistakes, than they will be affected by the mistakes themselves. If you are able to really believe this, then making any changes that are necessary should be a bit easier for you to do.

If these thoughts and ideas are new and seem foreign to you, and yet you are willing to try them out, then I encourage you to take a deep breath, grit your teeth, and risk asking forgiveness next time you blow it with your kids. If these are new and uncomfortable ideas for you, they will no doubt be difficult at first. If it is necessary, force yourself to say the words, even though at first those words might feel like you're speaking a foreign language. In fact, hearing those words from you might at first seem like a foreign language to your kids as well.

Seriously consider that when you apologize to your kids and ask for their forgiveness, you are actually strengthening and encouraging their ability to trust. And as they develop an ability to trust, they are more likely to develop a healthy and appropriate trust of others.

If we are able to consistently portray a humble, vulnerable behavior in our relationship with our kids, then we will provide for them a model to follow and to learn from. Most of us want our kids to grow up capable of admitting when they are wrong, and willing to acknowledge when they have made a mistake. We want them to acquire a sense of humility that allows them to admit their weaknesses. The process of teaching these values begins with us—their parents—and it is accomplished best by modeling such behavior ourselves; to do so does not demonstrate weakness, but rather, strength.

## WHAT'S THE BOTTOM LINE?

Pride, competition, and fear are three of the major stumbling blocks that make it difficult for most of us to apologize to our kids. And how much more difficult it is to actually ask if they will forgive us! It's bad enough that they already know we are not perfect, but for us to acknowledge our short comings and to actually ask them to forgive us for our imperfections is a risk that many of us find difficult to take.

But when we are willing to humble ourselves to the point of admitting our faults and weaknesses, we model for our kids the importance of doing the same—not only in their relationship with us, but in their friendships with others as well. And it will be their willingness to do so that will help strengthen and deepen the bonds with others throughout their lives.

We take a difficult risk when we say to our kids, "I'm sorry, will you forgive me?" But as a result of our efforts to humble ourselves, we strengthen and improve their capacity to trust us. Our kids will remember and be affected far more by how we respond after we make a mistake than they will by the actual mistakes we make. If this is true (and of course I believe that it is!), then the mistakes we make provide us the opportunity to guide and shape them in ways that will positively impact them for the rest of their lives.

## Discussion Questions:

1. Were your parents willing to apologize to you when they made mistakes?

2. Did their being willing to (or not) cause you to respect them, to disrespect them, or was there no affect at all?

3. Are you usually able to say you are sorry to your kids when you are wrong?

4. When you do apologize and ask forgiveness, what response do you usually get from them?

5. Do you think that your ability or inability to ask forgiveness makes it easier (or more difficult) for them to do the same?

6. When you have made a mistake do you have any fears about apologizing to your kids (loss of respect, control, being too vulnerable, having your humility used against you, etc.)?

*"Infants, kids, and adults alike, all need healthy and appropriate physical contact with others."*

# QUESTION #12:

## *Am I physical with my kids?*

WHEN WE THINK OF OUR NEED for physical touch and intimacy, what usually comes to mind first is our need for the kind of touch that is sexual in nature. While it is certainly true that sexual touch and intimacy is a need that we humans have in common, we also share a very strong and innate need to be touched in a nonsexual way as well.

Communication by way of touch is so powerful that it can convey warmth, compassion, understanding, support, acceptance, a sense of being heard, and a lot more of what feels good to the one being touched; it can also communicate disdain, rejection, disappointment and a great deal more that can hurt. It is ironic, that the touch we receive from others can create some of life's most pleasurable moments for us, or it has the potential of resulting in some of the most horrific experiences we could ever possibly imagine.

The role our verbal communication plays in the development of our kids' was addressed previously in Chapter 2. As important as our verbal communication is in shaping their lives, our physical touch is another powerful form of communication that may be heard more loudly than what we communicate verbally. Our touch has the potential of either helping them prosper, or it can interfere with their healthy growth and development.

In addition to the improper use of touch, that we unfortunately hear so much about these days, there is also the potential for misunderstanding the well-meaning motivations of positive touch. It is this possibility for misunderstanding that has led our society to overreact and to sexualize almost any form of touching children. Physical touch from others may be offered with the best of motivations and intentions, and yet it may be misinterpreted by the one being touched.

As a result of the possibility of misunderstanding and the consequences that can result, our society tends to err in the direction of withholding physical contact from young children all together. Just recently in a Southern California town, a 12-year-old was suspended for hugging another student. His actions resulted in suspension because it violated the school's recently instated "no touch" policy. This is not exceptional, since many public agencies that work with children have begun to adopt this policy as a means of protecting both workers and children alike.

Without arguing the necessity of such policies, the results of this increasing fear tends to leave the family as the only perceived safe and appropriate source of the physical contact that kids so desperately need. (Sadly, touch within the boundaries of the family is not always safe and appropriate either). Since we parents are becoming the primary source of safe touch for our kids, it is all the more important that we not only place a priority on communicating with them verbally, but communicating with them in a physical manner as well.

Additionally, it is a widely held assumption, that as little kids grow older they no longer need physical touch from others. Nothing could be further from the truth. Of all the needs we humans have in common, none is as minimized as is our continued need for the non-sexual touch from others even as we grow older. While it is commonly argued that touch is a greater necessity for our young children as they grow and develop than it is for us older folk, none of us really ever outgrows our need to be touched by others. So as our infants grow to be toddlers and our toddlers grow to be adolescents and then teenagers, their need for physical contact remains. They may need it in different ways, but they still need to be touched.

Although it is not a scientific study, an important observation was made in an orphanage just outside London in the mid-1940s. What happened, by pure accident, demonstrates and supports this idea of just how important touch is to the human experience. World War II was in full swing and as is the case with all wars, the number of orphans was growing at an alarming rate. As a result of the increased numbers of children being left homeless, this "home" for orphaned babies was established.

It was actually little more than a warehouse that kept babies, who had lost their parents, safe and fairly well nourished until a permanent home could be found. Although it served an important purpose—as a place where these babies and toddlers were given the physical care like clothing, food, and shelter they needed— little importance was placed on their emotional well-being. The staff was no doubt short handed, and it was most likely all they could do just to attend to the many physical needs that were most obvious. In fairness too, they also did not understand what we do today about the emotional needs of infants and how those needs relate to their physical stimulation.

At this particular orphanage the mortality rate of the infants was 50 percent. You read it correctly. An astounding one half of all babies brought to the orphanage, died within a year and a half of their arrival! Despite the fact that all of the babies were being well-cared for, as far as their physiological needs were concerned, the alarming death rate persisted. The cause of death was usually described as "maramus," a Greek word which refers to infantile atrophy where an infant literally wastes away.

It is not clear who thought of it first but someone came up with the idea of physically touching the babies more. Prior to this suggestion, each baby had its own crib and was basically left alone except when it came time for either a change of diapers, when they had a medical need, or when it came time to feed them. Even when they were fed, they were usually handed a bottle and expected to feed themselves if they were able to do so.

The person who decided to touch the babies more must have recognized the mistake of physically connecting with the children only when they were fed, clothed or medically attended to. It must have seemed like a ridiculous idea at the time, and was probably not welcomed with great enthusiasm, given the shortage of time, energy and staffing.

Nonetheless, the order was given to all workers—from the director on down to the janitor—were to reach down and stroke or gently touch every baby any time they passed a crib during the course of their work day. They were not required to pick them up or spend any significant amount of time being physical; they were asked to touch them. The apparent result of this new mandate was astonishing. Within a two-year period, the mortality rate of infants brought to the orphanage dropped from 50 percent to 15 percent. I suppose one could argue the case for coincidence, since it was not a scientific study, but given what we have learned about touch in the past fifty years, doesn't it stand to reason that there just may have been a relationship between the babies being touched and the decrease in mortality rate?

If you have ever witnessed the birth of an animal, you have no doubt seen the efforts of a weary mother licking her newborn in order to actually "jump start" its little motor. If the mother does not give this immediate physical attention, then her off-spring will usually be weaker and less healthy, if it lives at all. It must be touched and it must be stimulated if it is to thrive—or even survive—physically. The importance of the mother's touch provides some insight into the fact that it is usually the last born in a litter, the one that normally receives the least physical attention from an already exhausted mother that either dies, or if it lives, becomes the runt of the litter.

## SOME OF THE BENEFITS OF BEING PHYSICAL WITH OUR KIDS

It has been found that the brain size in infants who have received more physical stimulation early in their lives is larger, while the brain of those babies who have received very little physical contact is usually somewhat smaller. Through brain scans, it has not only been determined that physically stimulated babies develop larger brains, but that there is less space between their brain spheres as well. These physiological differences in brain mass were present despite the fact that nutritionally, all of the babies studied had similar and adequate diets.

This brain development study provides strong evidence to support the importance of physical touch for the healthy development of our kids physiologically, but their physical and mental well-being is only one factor that is affected by touch from others. While it is not as easy to prove or demonstrate, it is likely that the development of social and relational skills in our kids are positively affected by healthy and steady doses of physical touch. Can you think of anyone in your circle of friends who is healthy and well-adjusted that dislikes being touched, who stiffens when someone reaches out to them physically? Certainly there are exceptions, but generally, a willingness to touch and be touched by others, more often than not, accompanies a healthy sense of well-being.

Infants, kids, and adults alike, all have a need for emotional attachment and healthy physical connection to others. When we attach to our kids through touch and physical responsiveness, they are more likely to grow up to be adults who are capable of making healthy and appropriate attachments with others.

On the other hand, kids who are deprived of early physical attachment and stimulation are either more likely to eventually be adults who physically insulate themselves from others, or they may—due to physical deprivation—be addicted to the physical touch from others and never seem to get enough.

Learning to trust the physical touch from others helps strengthen their ability and willingness to trust in other ways as well. Consequently, kids who are touched in healthy and appropriate ways will be less likely to grow up fearful and untrusting of physical and emotional relationships with others.

## WHAT'S A PARENT TO DO?

As babies grow from infancy to childhood, and eventually into teenagers—when, where and how we touch them changes. In fact sometime during their childhood years, they will no doubt go through a stage where they don't want to be touched at all! But it is likely their need to be touched physically—perhaps not as frequently and in different ways—will eventually resurface and it will once again become an important part of your relationship with them.

Watch for creative and spontaneous ways of connecting physically with your kids. Of course, this is easier when they are infants and toddlers, than it will be later on when they are older. But while they are still infants, rub their heads, hold them close, pat them on the back, kiss and hug them on a regular basis.

When they are playing on the floor or lying in their crib, make it a point to reach down and simply touch them, just as was done in the London orphanage described earlier. Remember that while they may not respond, you are nonetheless stimulating them in a way that will positively impact them both emotionally and physically for their lifetime.

As your kids grow older, remember that although they still need physical touch, they may no longer appreciate or need it in the same way. That's right, someday it will no longer be "cool" to be physically close to Mom and Dad, and it will be apparent that your attempts at being physical—at least in the same ways—are no longer acceptable to them. And it is important to remember that their temporary indifference has nothing to do with their love, respect, or care for you.

As they begin to shun your attempts at being physical, respect their need for space and their resistance to what not so long ago they seemed to want and even crave from you. It may be at this point that you will have to accept any "hit and run" touches you are able to pull off in passing. And accepting their changing needs for physical affection is another way to convey your respect for them.

## What's the bottom line?

Physical touch from others is a necessary ingredient for the nurturing of our kids if they are to grow and develop physically and emotionally. Although the touch from others may no longer seem to be an absolute necessity as they grow older, it can safely be said that they (we) never outgrow their need for the physical touch of others.

When we are physical with our kids, we provide them with a foundation for emotional and social health and well-being. There is also evidence which suggests that healthy physical contact even increases brain size and the ability to learn.

Being physical with your kids increases the prospect of their being able to enjoy appropriate physical relationships with others well into their adult lives. And who knows, you may even discover and satisfy some of your own dormant needs for physical contact. While your need for physical contact may decrease with age, you will never completely outgrow your need for it.

## DISCUSSION QUESTIONS:

1.  Were your parents physical with you when you were young?

2.  What affect do you think their being physical (or not) has had on you as an adult?

3.  Are you physical with your kids?

4.  If you are, what forms does your being physical take?

5.  How do they respond to your being physical (or not) with them?

6.  Do you need to improve your efforts at showing affection with your kids?

7.  What are some possible ways you can try to be more physical with them?

*"Kids who are able to laugh at themselves once in a while tend to have more self-respect and self-confidence than do those who take themselves more seriously."*

# QUESTION #13:

*Are my kids able to laugh at themselves?*

THE INTERNET PROVIDES VOLUMES of information about the benefit of laughter. There is no question that the physical and emotional well-being of people who laugh on a regular basis is significantly improved as a result. Laughter not only has a positive affect on blood pressure, stress, the immune system and our general outlook on life, there is scientific evidence to suggest that it actually improves brain functions as well. The list of benefits go on and on; suffice it to say, there is little debate that laughter is very good for our emotional and physical health and well-being.

It is interesting, however, that a search for information on laughter leads to very little regarding the importance of our learning to laugh at ourselves. And yet, teaching our kids to do just that is one of the very important roles we parents must play in their lives. Not only is laughter an ingredient often found in the make up of physically and emotionally healthy people, our ability to laugh at ourselves is of importance as well.

Think of a person you enjoy being with and are drawn to. For some reason you just like being around them and you would like to spend more time with them. Maybe you know them well or perhaps you have just observed them from a distance. What are three or four personality traits or characteristics that attract you to them? What makes them stand out as someone you are glad you know or would like to know better? Most likely, one of the reasons you are drawn to this person is your observation that they don't take themselves too seriously, and that they don't mind having a good laugh at their own expense.

Most emotionally healthy people can laugh at themselves— and as a result, other people want to be around them. When they put their foot in their mouth at a social gathering, trip over themselves when trying to explain an idea, or goof up in some other way, they can recover by being the first to poke fun at themselves. Usually others join in and a good laugh is had by all.

Now think for a moment of a person who you are not attracted to. You may even avoid them when you see them coming your way. Is the person you have in mind able to laugh at themselves or do they have the tendency to take themselves more seriously than they should? They may have other qualities that you want to avoid as well, but chances are among their unattractive characteristics is also the inability and unwillingness to laugh at themselves.

Emotionally healthy people know that occasionally having a good laugh at their own expense does not mean they are dumb, a failure, or inferior. Being able and willing to laugh at yourself means you know you aren't perfect—but for a healthy, well-adjusted person, that's OK.

## How kids learn to laugh at themselves

New born babies probably do come equipped at birth with a certain capacity for laughter. If you have ever observed an infant around the second month of life, you may have noticed that it is around this time that they gradually begin to smile. After a few more months of life, they actually begin to show signs of laughter.

This begins so early in life that it appears we are all born with an ability to laugh.

However, I believe the freedom to actually laugh at ourselves is a learned response that must be taught. Kids who are able to poke good humored fun at themselves must learn to do so. If this is true, from whom are they most likely to learn the fine art of laughing at themselves? Their ability and willingness to do so must evolve through experiences and observations, and it is a process that begins at an early age that is largely a result of watching and observing Mom and Dad and how they react.

Have you ever noticed how a baby just learning to stand reacts when he falls? He has just made a first effort at pulling himself up by holding on to the coffee table when all of a sudden he comes crashing to the floor right back where he began. Usually that little baby will look around to see how all those big people around him are responding to his "failed" attempt to stand. And typically he will take the lead from those around him to determine what the appropriate response might be. His little "sponge-like brain" seems to be thinking, "How am I supposed to react to this? I don't know whether to laugh or cry! Should I feel foolish, or is this funny, and should it be OK with me that it is funny?" If our response is horror, as if they've just permanently damaged themselves, then they will learn to respond more seriously even though no harm was done.

If we make a habit of laughing at some of the little goofs our kids make, then they will be more likely to laugh as well. And as they grow older, by watching us and our reactions to not only their goofs, flaws, and imperfections, but to our own as well, they will conclude that there is value and wisdom in learning to laugh at themselves once in a while.

If we react to their goof-ball mistakes (which often really are funnier than they are tragic) with disappointment or sadness and as if they have once again let us down, then they too will learn to be disappointed, rather than take their imperfections and themselves less seriously. If we smile and laugh a little in the midst of our helping them correct their mistake, then they too will learn to take themselves less seriously. As in so many other experiences in life, our kids learn how to respond by watching us and how we react.

How seriously do we take ourselves? Are we able to chuckle at our own trivial mistakes, or do we model a seriousness that sends a message of self-depreciation rather than self-acceptance? Are we able to poke a little fun at our own imperfections, or when we fall short do we consistently ridicule ourselves?

We will model the value and pleasure of occasionally finding humor in our own imperfections and flaws when our kids see us laugh at ourselves and our mistakes. When they see that we are able to find humor in our own shortcomings, and to take ourselves less seriously, they will be more likely and able to do the same. If we are free enough to poke light-hearted fun at ourselves from time to time, then they too will be more likely to do the same.

It is interesting—sometimes downright painful—to watch kids playing in a group. It doesn't take long before an important difference between the most popular kids and the "runt of the litter" begins to appear. If you are able to observe them for an extended period it will usually become clear that the most well-liked kids are usually the ones who are able to laugh at themselves when they've blown it or done something "dumb." They do not take themselves or their minor errors too seriously.

In that same play group you will probably find at least one playmate that is more likely than the others to be ridiculed or picked on. Once again, if you watch long enough, you will likely see the children who are unable to laugh at themselves and who take their every move so seriously are the ones who will be picked on most by the others. It is largely their inability to laugh at themselves that makes them an easy target for the others.

## WHAT'S A PARENT TO DO?

Certainly, it is important to draw a distinction between laughing with our kids and making fun of our kids. Ridicule has no place here and is not a part of teaching the fine art of taking themselves less seriously. In fact, some parents are under the impression that their responses toward their kids are appropriate when in fact they are using ridicule, and laughing at the expense of their kids.

Since laughter plays such an important role in our raising kids who are healthy and balanced, it is important to incorporate as much of it as possible into our relationship with them. At first glance, this might not seem like such a difficult task, but for many parents who are caught up in making a living and dealing with all of the more difficult realities of life, laughter has become a lost art and not a behavior that comes naturally.

Make an intentional effort around the dinner table to use a little humor. And if you aren't eating together most nights, make an effort to do so! While telling jokes or funny stories may not always fit into the category of teaching your kids to laugh at themselves, it does teach them to laugh, and laughter of any kind exercises the laugh muscle. This particular emotional muscle seems to be one that is seriously underused these days! Exercising the laugh muscle will also go a long way in helping them to see the humor in more of life's circumstances.

Talk about one funny thing that happened in everyone's day. It may be something they observed, or it might be something they did. Encourage them once in awhile to "admit" to a dumb or silly thing they did that day. And remember that they will be keenly aware of your reaction to the "dumb" thing they confess.

Look for ways to model this behavior, by laughing at yourself, and letting them in on what you've done. This will help them to develop the ability to turn the potential for shame into humor.

Try taking the lead once in awhile at actually laughing at them. This is always risky and we need to be cautious that our attempts are not seen as ridicule. But often—just as with the baby attempting to stand for the first time—they are looking to you for a better handle on how to respond.

## What's the bottom line?

There are many qualities that make certain people attractive; the ability to laugh at ones self is one of them. These people have learned that when they laugh at themselves, others usually do the same and what might otherwise have been an embarrassing event is instead turned into a humorous one.

We are all born with the ability and capacity for laughter. But being able to laugh at ourselves when it is appropriate seems to be an acquired trait that is learned after birth and as a result of observing and modeling all those people around us early in our lives.

Among the many duties and responsibilities we have as parents, an important priority should be developing within our kids the self-respect and confidence it takes to laugh at themselves. When they are able to laugh at themselves, then others will laugh too—but they will be laughing with them, rather than at them.

## DISCUSSION QUESTIONS:

1. Were you able to laugh at yourself when you were young and growing up?

2. Did your parents play a role in your learning that it was ok (or not) to laugh at yourself?

3. Are your kids usually able to appropriately laugh at themselves?

4. What role have you played as a parent in their learning that it is ok (or not) to laugh at themselves?

5. If your kids are able to laugh at themselves, can you see ways that it benefits them in social settings with their peers?

6. If they are more likely to take themselves too seriously, how does this characteristic play out for them socially?

"*If we encourage our kids to ignore, deny and cover up their feelings and emotions, they will be less able to control them.*"

## Question #14:

*Do I teach my kids that it is ok to have their feelings regardless of what those feelings are?*

CAN YOU THINK OF any physical object that simply ceases to exist because we have covered it up, hidden or ignored it? When we deny that something exists because it is either unsightly or unacceptable, have we succeeded in making it disappear or go away? Unless a magician is involved, it is very unlikely. And even then it is just an illusion and the audience has been fooled. Yet when we humans deny and cover up our undesired feelings and emotions, it is easy to assume that we have succeeded at somehow making them go away. In so doing, we conclude they will no longer be a bother to us. It is unfortunate, but nothing could be further from the truth. Like the magician's audience, when we deny our feelings and emotions, we too have been fooled.

When we maintain a pattern of emotional denial and cover-up, the object of our denial will eventually resurface. And when it does, our feelings will create problems—not only for us, but for those around us as well. Unfortunately and ironically, those we are closest to are often the ones most affected when our buried emotions surface.

Emotions that our kids deny and cover up have an affect on them as well. Just as our denial is likely to come back to haunt us, theirs too will at some time, in some direction, and in some form come out. They may not come out until their teen years, or perhaps they may lay dormant and surface in their marriage relationship. Although we can never know when, what form, or in what direction their denied emotions may come out, it is a sure thing that they will come out, and when they do there will be problems.

Denied feelings and emotions may surface in an external and explosive direction (toward others), or they may implode (be aimed toward themselves). They may take on a new look, so to speak. For instance, when kids are consistently denied the freedom of expressing and sorting out their anger in a proper and safe manner, their anger may show up later in some other emotion. Hurt is often the emotion that replaces denied anger. Likewise, hurt that is not allowed expression often shows up later in the form of anger.

A good example is what we often refer to as "raging bulls" in this world. We have all known at least one during our lifetime. This is the person who, when we see them coming we just get out of their way because we've seen their short fuse and raging temper. Although they are very quick to anger and explosive behaviors, the real emotion that may lie beneath all that extreme volatility is hurt. Often that angry person was unable to express their hurt for fear of being labeled a "crybaby" or a complainer. Perhaps they feared being teased about being too sensitive; wanting to avoid that danger, they denied their hurt and stuffed it way down, only to surface as anger. This emotional trade may occur early in a person's development or at can lay dormant and show up at a later date.

Most of us have also known a "hurt little puppy dog" or two. Often these people who whimper their way through life are internally more angry than they are hurt. Perhaps as kids it was not safe to express their anger, so they learned to stuff that emotion and trade it in for the safer alternative of being hurt and fragile. And for many angry kids, acting hurt rather than owning their anger is not only the safer emotion, but it might also result in their receiving care, attention or rescuing they are unable to get any other way.

The denial and cover-up of feelings does not always lead to this reversal of emotions. It is also possible that the results of stuffed and ignored emotions may show up in an extreme version of the original emotion that was not expressed. In other words, all raging bulls are not expressing denied hurt or other emotions that were not allowed. It may be that their current rage is the result of built up anger that was not allowed safe and appropriate expression the first time around. Likewise, all hurt puppy dogs are not necessarily a result of denied anger, but may be reacting to having never been free to communicate their childhood hurts.

When we humans consistently deny the existence of our negative emotions and feelings (fear, anger, hurt and more), we are far more likely to be out of touch with our positive emotions (love, joy, happiness, pleasure, etc) as well. This may provide as explanation as to why so many adults seem to live "flat line lives," showing little expression of happiness or joy. Our kids are no exception to this. When they are taught and encouraged to deny and cover up their negative emotions, eventually they may have less access to their positive emotions as well.

Although they may seem somewhat extreme, the above examples are suggested for the purpose of making this important point: We must allow and encourage our kids to express their feelings, and to encourage them to do so in a proper and acceptable fashion. If we do not, then their emotional health and well-being will be compromised.

When we give our kids the freedom to appropriately express their feelings, we give them a greater degree of control over those feelings. It is easier for us parents to encourage their expressing them when we understand that human feelings and emotions are neither good, nor are they bad. They just are. But what we do with their feelings can be good, and what they do with them can also be bad. This is why it is so important that they own them, that they face them, and that they take the responsibility to be in control of them. Without understanding and acknowledging them, there will be no controlling them.

Suppose you asked a doctor to look at a suspicious growth that has suddenly appeared on your arm. After completing the examination, he tells you that the growth is cancer and that something has to be done in order to prevent its having an adverse impact on your physical health and well-being. Rather than taking the doctor's advice, you simply place a band-aid over it and begin the process of denying the frightening fact that the life- threatening tumor exists. In so doing, you may have given yourself a more pleasant day—denial has a way of doing that—but ultimately you have allowed what you have denied to have a greater and unacceptable control over you.

It is the same with emotions: what we deny will control us. And it is only as our kids learn to face and acknowledge their feelings, that they will be able to exercise the necessary and appropriate controls over them. It is understandable that as parents we might want to stifle many of their emotions. The temptation to do so is often because we fear that if they were free to express their feelings, they might act on them. This is certainly an understandable concern, but the false assumption in this reasoning is that if our kids acknowledge and express their feelings, then they will be more likely to act on them.

It usually works in the very opposite way. Our kids will be far less likely to act inappropriately when they understand and are able to acknowledge their feelings and emotions. The more they understand them, the more likely they will be to verbalize them in an appropriate manner. And it is this awareness and appropriate expression of their feelings and emotions that leads to controlling what they do with them.

## WHAT'S A PARENT TO DO?

There are many ways we may discourage our kids from owning and identifying their feelings and emotions. These are but a few examples:

"You don't really hate your teacher. You're just frustrated."
Response: "If you say so, I guess I'm not angry after all."
"You shouldn't be hurt just because your friend lies to you. Just ignore her."
Response: "I guess it's not OK to be hurt, so I will ignore and deny that I am."
"How could you possibly feel lonely? You have so many friends."
Response; "I guess I must not feel lonely. . . . then what do I feel?"
"Oh, you aren't really mad. I think you must just be disappointed."
Response: "I sure feel mad, but if you say so, I must not be."
"How could you be angry with dad when you love him so much?"
Response: "I guess if you love someone, you can never be mad at them. Since I love him, I must not really be mad."

These are just a few of the subtle ways that we may train our kids to avoid, ignore, and deny their feelings and emotions. Rather than encouraging and participating in the cover up, it is important that we help them identify, understand, express, and then control their emotions.

Once again the responsibility falls on us parents to teach our kids that while it is ok for them to feel like poking their friend in the nose, it is not alright to do it. It is important to teach them that while it is ok and maybe even reasonable to feel like getting even when they have been wronged, it is not acceptable to act on that feeling.

We must help them see that while it is acceptable—even understandable—to feel like never again talking to a friend who has hurt them, it is not ok to follow through with their urge. We must allow and enable them—and without fear of retaliation—to tell Dad that they think he's unfair because he took their bike away. They must also learn that it is not alright to scream it in the middle of the grocery store (or to say it in a disrespectful way anywhere, for that matter).

It must be ok for our kids to say, "You don't love me and you never did!" It is not acceptable to say it while taking the air out of your tires as a means of getting even and driving home their point.

We must allow them to be angry because their new little sister is no longer a novelty and it is finally clear to them that she is here to stay; it is also our responsibility to teach them that it is not ok to express those feelings by placing her out on the curb to be picked up with the trash!

## WHAT'S THE BOTTOM LINE?

Feelings and emotions are not good, nor are they bad. They just are. What does earn the label of either good or bad is what we do with the emotions we have. Of all the tasks and responsibilities we have as a parent, none is more important than helping our kids identify, understand, respect, and then control their emotions. It is tempting to teach them that the best way to control their feelings and emotions is to deny that they exist; that the best way to have impulse control over their behaviors is to keep their feelings and emotions inside and to themselves. Nothing could be further from the truth.

It is essential that our kids learn to be in control of their emotions. All it takes is a quick read of any local newspaper to be reminded that there are far too many people in our world who do not know how to control their emotions.

We can best help our kids develop an appropriate control over their emotions by actually allowing and encouraging them to appropriately express themselves, regardless of what their emotions are. Only then will we help them know what to do with those emotions and how to maintain a healthy control over them.

## DISCUSSION QUESTIONS:

1. Were your mom and dad a good model for appropriately expressing feelings and emotions?

2. When you were growing up, were you encouraged to appropriately express your feelings and emotions?

3. What sign or indication did you get from your mom or dad that led you to believe it was either ok (or not) to have your feelings and emotions?

4. As a parent do you encourage your kids to express their feelings in appropriate ways regardless of what their feelings might be?

5. Do your kids ever behave in a way that suggests they may be acting out feelings and emotions they do not feel free to express in any other way?

6. In what ways might you convey to your kids that it is ok to have their feelings and emotions as long as they are expressed appropriately?

*"It is important to encourage our kids to help, even though when they do they may at first not be of much help at all."*

# Question # 15:

## *Do I encourage my kids to help?*

WHAT PARENT HAS NOT at times said to their very young kids who were ready, willing and eager to help with some task, "Let me do it so we won't be here all day," or "Let me do it so it gets done right," or "You're making this harder for me. Move out of the way so I can get the job done."

And how many of us parents of adolescents and teenagers have made comments to them like, "You never lift a finger to help around here. All I am to you is a meal ticket," or

"Do you think that I'm the only one around here who is capable of helping?," or "Why is it that every time I ask you to help out a little, I get a groan and a dirty look from you?"

What often lies behind such complaints from parents of adolescents and teenagers is a little kid who at one time was not allowed or encouraged to help. When they wanted to be a part of things by helping, they seemed to be more in the way than they were a help. So slowly but surely, that little kid faded into the background when there were chores to be done, tasks to be accomplished. After all, it seemed like Mom and Dad preferred it that way since they could get more done, do it right the first time, and not have to take the time to instruct and encourage. But as they grew older, the kids kind of liked it that way too.

Adolescents and teenagers do not all of a sudden blossom into helpers with good attitudes. They are trained, encouraged, expected, and given opportunities to become helpers. They are designed by us very early in their lives to be capable and to have a willing spirit in the midst of their helping. And it is largely through our efforts at involving them in chores and tasks, when they are young and not much help at all, that will create their desire to help later on. In the long run, our patience and tolerance will lead to a more willing and capable spirit when finally their help really is needed.

Remember from Chapter 1, that our young kids have sponge-like brains that don't think and process in the way ours does. Unlike an adult brain, children are more likely to absorb, without questioning, what it hears, what it sees, and what it is told. So when our very young children are not encouraged and instructed in the midst of their efforts to help, their likely response and conclusion over time will be something like, "I must not be of much help," or "It seems like I'm always in the way," or "I must not have much to offer." These and other conclusions like them have become adolescent and teenage patterns of thinking and behaving that have come back to haunt countless parents throughout the ages!

It goes without saying that if we ask our young kids to help with just about any task around the house, that whatever it is we are trying to accomplish, it will take us longer and quite likely will not turn out as good as it would had we just done it ourselves. However, by now you know all too well, our kids are not a "finished product," but rather, a "product in process." They are in the process of becoming and that process requires trial and error, successes and failures. We all know this intellectually, but it is easy to forget. One way of helping them in this process of developing skills and a helpful spirit, is to allow and encourage them to participate in tasks and chores that might actually be easier for us to accomplish if we just did them ourselves.

## WHY ENCOURAGE OUR YOUNG KIDS TO HELP BEFORE THEY ARE MUCH HELP AT ALL?

There are many good reasons to encourage our kids to fumble their way through helping us, even though the return on our investment is not immediate. Three reasons stand out as most important to consider: competence, a willing spirit, and a sense of significance.

## COMPETENCE

When we allow, encourage, and sometimes even insist that our kids help, we play a significant role in creating and developing competence in them. Most adolescents, teenagers and adults who know how to do a lot of things well have usually developed their skills through having had many life experiences. Two of the more important life experiences that help develop a sense of competence are helping and being involved at a young age, and learning through patient instruction.

There are many experiences we humans can have that help develop skills and competence. We can read a book, watch someone else, travel, and we can learn through instructions or lectures in the classroom. But there is no better way for our young kids to develop competence than through the "hands on" process of learning through doing while under the watchful eye of a loving instructor.

## A WILLING AND COOPERATIVE SPIRIT

I am reminded of a time when our oldest daughter, Ashley, was in sixth grade. One of her elective classes was called, "On Your Own." In this class, the students learned a variety of things like finances, cooking, and health principles. One day she came home and wanted to help make some apple turnovers. That was ok by her

Mom, so the process of making the world's best apple turn-over began.

Early on in the process, I could see that Ashley was taking some "creative freedom" in her efforts. Freedoms like, when the recipe called for one cup of flour, she added "about" a cup, one table-spoon of water became a "splash" of water from the tap. Her Mom took the time to explain the importance of being more accurate rather than approximate, but Ashley, being a student in "On Your Own," preferred to be . . . well, on her own.

It was very tempting for me to rush in and take over, demand-ing that we do things my way—the right way, of course. I was even tempted to declare that if she could not help in the way we wanted her to help, that she would not be allowed to be a part of the process.

Fortunately, my wife (as usual) had the better sense of the two of us, and after explaining the importance of being very accurate in following recipes, she backed off and let Ashley learn through her mistakes. Sure enough, those apple turnovers were not easily digested, nor chewed for that matter. (I recall privately having the idea of slapping a little varnish on each one and making door stops out of them. Fortunately, reason prevailed and I kept the idea to myself.) So Ashley learned in a practical way the importance of being precise when following a recipe.

If I had been in charge of that cooking adventure, we might have gotten the job done the right way in the first place, but I would have also interfered with her efforts to help, and would have deprived her of an important learning experience. We might have had a more edible end product, but she would not have learned as much through the process.

As Ashley grew into a teenager, she was almost always a ready helper and participant when it came to doing tasks and chores. She also followed recipes in precise fashion and even learned to bake a pretty mean apple turnover; so not only did she learn to have a willing spirit, she also developed a competence in the kitchen. As it turned out, not a great deal was lost—in fact a great deal was gained—in her first efforts at cooking.

Her willing spirit came about as a result of many other experiences in addition to the one cited here. But the point of this story is to suggest that our kids must be encouraged to help even though when they do, it may not be convenient, and furthermore, it may not even be a successful adventure as far as the task goes. But it is through such trial and error experiences that kids learn the skills and develop competence for a successful life.

## A sense of significance

There is a third goal that supports the notion of encouraging our kids to help at an early age. Kids who are a part of accomplishing tasks, chores and projects, grow up believing that they are a significant part of a team. And because of this team attitude, they feel more needed, and that their efforts and contributions matter.

Being a part of the family team helps kids grow up feeling good about themselves and what they have to offer. Because they are a piece of "the big picture" their feelings of significance and importance develops, and this in turn helps accomplish our goal of raising truly healthy kids. Without this sense of relevance that comes from helping and being a part of the family team, children can have a difficult time believing they have much worth or value as their world expands beyond the boundaries of their family experience.

## What's a parent to do?

The first word that comes to mind is patience. Without patience we might as well throw in the towel on this one. Remember that when going into a task or project—especially with our very young children—our patience will likely be tried and our desire for quality may sometimes be compromised.

Keep in mind that the most important goal and objective in letting our young kids help is not primarily to complete a task (although that would be nice, and you might be surprised how often the job will get done well, even if at a slower pace), but rather, to create an arena within which they can learn through new experiences.

Remember, the two key ingredients to children learning through trial and error experiences are encouragement and instruction rather than criticism and ridicule.


## WHAT'S THE BOTTOM LINE?

When we have a task or chore to do, our young kids may often be more in our way than they are a help to us. There are many benefits however, to encouraging them to help and to be involved at an early age.

When we encourage them to be a part of helping at a very early age, we instill and develop in them a generous dose of confidence and competence that will serve them well throughout their lives.

As a result of encouraging them to help before they are of much help at all, they will be more likely to develop a willing and cooperative attitude as they grow older. It is one thing to teach our kids the importance of helping and being a part of a team; it is yet another to develop within them a sincere and genuine desire to be of help to others.

By involving them at an early age, we help them internalize the belief that they are an important part of the family team.

In this day and age of long work hours, never-ending to-do lists, and the many other demands on our time, it is easy to lose sight of how important it is to encourage our kids to "help," even though when they do they are of little help to us. It is especially tempting to ignore the importance of involving them when it usually takes so much more of our energy to do so. The task and responsibility of raising great kids who like themselves and believe they have something to offer requires that we be willing to invest in this process.

## DISCUSSION QUESTIONS:

1.  When you were young did your parents encourage you to help, even before you were very much help to them?

2.  How did their attitude and approach about your helping shape you?

3.  Do you agree or disagree with the idea that it is important for very young kids to help, even before they are much help at all?

4.  If you now have young kids who want to help even though they really aren't much help at all to you, how do you respond to them and their efforts?

5.  How do your kids usually respond when they feel they have been a big help to you or even when they weren't?

6.  What are some specific ways you might be able to incorporate their helping into your family life?

"*The question is not whether our kids matter to us. Of course they do. The question is whether or not our actions and attitudes communicate to them that they do.*"

# Question #16:

## *Do my kids know they really matter?*

ANOTHER CHARACTERISTIC WE HUMAN beings have in common is our need to feel that we matter to those around us. We all want to believe that our presence, our opinions and our efforts somehow make a difference and that others care what we think. We seldom admit or talk about it, but we need to know that we matter so much to those around us that if we were gone, we'd be missed.

It is interesting to hear the response that many parents have when asked if their kids know they really matter to them. Most are at first taken back because of what seems to be a ridiculous question. Once they recover, their answer usually goes something like this: "Well of course my kids know I love them! They know beyond a shadow of doubt that I'd even die for them. I would give anything for them to be happy and they know it!"

Most of our kids do in fact know they are loved by us; they do know we would even give up our own lives for them. But as strange as it may seem, the fact that our kids know we love them and that we would sacrifice anything for their good, does not always translate into their believing that they really matter to us. Our loving them is a very good start but that's the easy part. Do they know they really matter?

As adults, most of us can look back on our childhood and feel that we were loved by our parents. Maybe at times they had strange ways of expressing that love, but somehow we knew they loved us. Even though we may have wondered from time to time if they really did, the vast majority of us can safely say that we did grow up in a family where our parents loved us. Many would in the same breath acknowledge that while they were indeed loved, there were times when whether they really did matter or not was in question.

But rather than taking my word for it, find out for yourself. Ask several of your closest friends if they were loved by their parents when they were kids. The vast majority will respond quickly that they were. Then ask those same people whether or not they also felt that they mattered. Did their thoughts, ideas, feelings, opinions, friends, schedules and desires really seem to be important to their parents? While certainly you will find those who grew up believing they did matter, you will also find a significant number who acknowledge that often they did not.

## BEING LOVED VS. KNOWING THEY MATTER

During the course of my private practice, I have treated very few people who did not believe their parents loved them in some way. In fact I can count on one hand (ok, maybe two hands) the number of times over the past 35 years of practice that I have heard someone say they grew up thinking they were not loved by their parents. But I have listened to hundreds and hundreds of people who, in spite of knowing they were loved, still grew up feeling that their presence in the family really didn't matter much.

This has led me to conclude that there are significant differences between the two and that it is possible for kids to grow up being loved, and at the same time convinced that their thoughts, their opinions, their schedules, their friends, their feelings and their emotions, really don't matter much to their parents. As important as being loved is to their emotional health and well-being, the positive effects of a parent's love can be diluted if it is not combined with a true and consistent message that they also matter. If they do not get the second message loud and clear, then simply loving them is not enough.

The question for us to consider is not whether our kids matter to us or not. Of course they do; they matter a great deal. The question is whether or not our behaviors and attitudes communicate that truth.

## When kids grow up believing they don't matter

When kids grow up believing they don't really matter, they are more likely to struggle with some form or degree of emotional and psychological difficulty. Their sense of insignificance can lead to a variety of issues that involve self doubt. On one hand, it may lead to very minor bouts with low self-esteem, depression and anxiety, or they may face far more serious difficulties. There are two broad and common categories that their struggles will typically fall into when they grow up believing they somehow don't matter.

## The underachiever

When kids grow up and out of their childhood home convinced that they don't much matter to those around them, chances are good that they will continue to be plagued by a lack of significance and importance. One possible outcome is their living flat and uneventful lives, venturing little and gaining even less; it may seem they determined to prove to those around them that they are insignificant. Kids like this become underachievers with very little self-confidence, who believe, "If I don't matter, then what I do with my life doesn't matter either."

## THE OVERACHIEVER

Ironically, another common behavior in this situation is the exact opposite direction of the underachiever described above. Having grown up convinced of their own insignificance, overachievers are on a mission, at any cost, to prove that they really do matter. They live their lives demanding others acknowledge how important they are. It is unfortunate but regardless of how hard they try to prove their worth through success, the belief that finally they really do matter usually eludes them.

## WHAT'S A PARENT TO DO?

The ways in which we act and respond toward our kids will either instill within them a real and lasting belief that they matter—or our words and actions will lead them to question their worth. Of course we know how much they matter to us, but that fact is irrelevant unless it is clearly and convincingly communicated. It is far more natural for us to love our kids (and it can come more automatically from us as well) than it is to show them just how much they matter, so here are several practical ways to accomplish this very important task:

Make a regular effort to find ways of showing your kids that you are interested in what they think. Ask them their opinion about certain ideas and issues.

If they are studying history, ask them their opinion on matters that pertain to what they are reading about. Don't ask as if you are testing to see what they know, or as if you have already formed an opinion. Ask them what they think as if their response might help you sort out your thoughts and ideas on the matter (and you shouldn't have to fake it. Who knows? They might just help give you a new perspective.)

They will believe they really matter when you ask them what they think about certain family or social issues. Knowing that you care about and respect their opinions goes a long way in showing that their presence in your life makes a difference.

Make it a habit of occasionally entering into their world, rather than constantly demanding that they follow you into yours. You can do this by following their lead at times, rather than insisting that they always fall in line with you just because you happen to be the adult. Be willing to do things the way they would like once in a while, rather than always expecting them to comply with your ways. There is room for both—and the ideal is a good balance between the two.

Find ways to show them that you value and appreciate their friends. To start, make sure their friends know they are welcome in your house. When they are around, treat them with respect and as a valued guest. Make a habit of following up on conversations regarding their friends. For instance, if you know your daughter's best friend is ill, remember to ask how he or she is doing.

Taking your child's schedule into consideration when planning trips or organizing any other family activities communicates to them that they matter. When they have an event or activity they would like to participate in, send the message that they matter by doing everything in your power to work around them and their social and athletic activities. Although it may not always work out, your sincere efforts to accommodate them will still send an important message.

Communicating to your kids that they matter does not mean that the world must revolve around them or that you must always do things their way. However, it does require making the effort to coordinate and at times, compromise your goals, ideas, needs and opinions. You will not always achieve this, but the important thing is your willingness to take your kids and their world into consideration.

A wise grandmother once related to me a conversation she had with her grown granddaughter. The granddaughter was telling her about a time when she was ten and had come to her house for a visit while her Grandma was in the midst of rearranging all the furniture and pictures in her living room: "You actually asked me—just a ten-year-old—how I thought the furniture should be arranged. You asked me Grandma, if I had any ideas about where the pictures would look best. Just asking my opinion made me feel special and that I really mattered. And when I came back several months later for a visit, and saw that my suggestions were still in place, I couldn't believe it!" That little ten-year-old girl felt important because her ideas really mattered to some big grown-up who was wise enough to take the time to ask her what she thought.

There are many other ways to convey this same idea:

"Brian, you know we are planning to be gone several weeks this summer. Is there a time that will not interfere with your soccer play-offs?

"I just read in the newspaper, Leanne, that a convicted killer got the death penalty. What are your thoughts on the morality of an 'eye for an eye'?"

"Your friend, Karen, seemed sad when she was here last night. Is she ok?"

"We've always eaten right at 6 p.m., but that doesn't seem to be working out as well for you and your volleyball schedule. Would eating a little later help you?"

"Scott, we are thinking very seriously about moving to another house. Do you have any thoughts about that idea? What are the pros and cons for you?"

Considering the needs of kids to this degree does not sit well with some parents. Often, the feeling is that such an open minded attitude will give away too much of the authority that should belong to the parent. But taking into consideration your kids' needs and ideas does not mean that you have now established a democratic system of family life where everyone must have an equal vote.

Taking into consideration their needs, thoughts, ideas and opinions does not necessarily mean you must conform to what they expect or want. And there is certainly room to disagree and to even turn down suggestions or requests in a way that does not take away from their feeling that their thoughts, feelings and opinions really are important to you. You must still maintain veto power, but if they consistently see your genuine interest in them and consideration of their needs, ideas, and opinions, you will have succeeded in showing them that they matter.

## What's the bottom line?

Our kids do need our unconditional love, and it would not be a stretch of the truth to say that their knowing we love them is a necessary ingredient in our relationship if they are to thrive. But as important as our love for them is, they must also know clearly and consistently just how much they matter to us as well. Our love for them does not automatically and necessarily satisfy their need know they also matter to us.

We communicate how much their presence in our lives matters to us when we ask what they think about various issues, or seek their opinion on ideas we have. We also communicate that they matter to us when we show a genuine interest in their friends. When we take into consideration their schedule and their desires when planning a family outing and vacation, we send the message that beyond loving them, their desires and needs matter to us as well.

None of this is meant to suggest that your kids must always have an equal vote (although once in a while might be nice), but it does mean that you care what they think, that you want to take their needs into consideration when making family decisions, and that what is important to them is important to you—even when you don't agree with them.

There are many undesirable results that may occur when kids grow up questioning their importance in the lives of others. There are two in particular that are the most common:

First, an underachiever who has become convinced that since they don't matter, then life doesn't matter much either, so there is no point in trying; second, an overachiever who is motivated by the need to prove their worth to everyone around them, all the time. Regardless of how hard they try, it never seems to be enough to convince themselves that they do matter.

A challenging but rewarding responsibility we parents have that goes well beyond simply loving our kids is showing them just how much their thoughts, emotions, opinions, friends, schedules, ideas and needs matter to us. While loving them comes naturally for most of us, communicating just how deeply we value their presence may take an extra and intentional effort on our part.

## Discussion Questions:

1. Taking into consideration what you have just read here, did you grow up feeling that you really mattered to your parents?

2. In what ways are you affected today as a result of how you grew up feeling about your importance in the family?

3. Does how you grew up feeling about yourself and whether you mattered influence the messages you now give your kids about their importance?

4. In what specific ways do you show your kids that they matter to you?

5. Do you feel that your kids know they matter to you (their feelings, friends, opinions, schedule, etc)?

6. What are some ways of communicating to your kids how much they really matter to you?

*"We earn the right to be heard by our kids by first listening to what they have to say."*

# QUESTION #17:

## *Do I listen to my kids?*

SOMETIME AROUND THE LATE 1960's, a new and creative social service was offered in the San Francisco area. It began small and operated out of an unimpressive store front. Above the door was a sign that read: "The Listening Ear." On the same sign was a roughly sketched image of an ear and a posted price of $10 per half hour session. The purpose of the service was to provide a place where people could be listened to. During the early months this listening business was in operation, there was a sign taped to the glass door. It read something like this:

Help Wanted
We need people who can listen.
No experience necessary.
Social workers, professional counselors, graduate students in
Psychology and anyone with wisdom to share need not apply.

Apparently, they were looking to hire people who could listen rather than dispense information, give advice or talk about their own life experiences. Within a couple of months there was a long waiting list of customers who apparently just wanted to be heard, just wanted to be listened to and were willing to pay what was, at the time fairly big bucks, for the service. The success of this listening business suggests what way down deep, most of us already know, and that is that we human beings want to be heard and understood by someone more than we want to be given advice. (Those of us in the helping profession, take note.)

When we think of effective communicators, we usually picture someone who has an ability to speak and clearly convey their thoughts and ideas to another person. Certainly to be able to do so is a necessity for anyone who fancies themselves a good communicator. But is it the most important characteristic of gifted communicators? Not according to The Listening Ear in San Francisco.

When parents are asked if they spend much time listening to their kids, many will respond something like this: "Of course I do! It seems like I'm always talking to them." It is easy for us to confuse listening—really hearing what it is they have to say—with talking to (or at) them. We tend to bundle talking and listening together and then call the combination communication. Then it would follow that it doesn't really matter which we are doing; as long as we are engaged in either talking or listening, we may believe that real communication is taking place.

But sometimes our kids just need to be heard rather than talked to. And yet, it is easy for our own needs to be heard to compete with and take priority over our efforts to just quietly listen to them. This is not always due to a selfish need to dominate and may often be a result of feeling the pressure of, "so little time" and the necessity of getting across as much wisdom, information, thoughts and ideas as possible, in an effort to influence them. It is natural to feel that we must take advantage of any and every moment we have to teach and instruct. While what we have to say is of great importance over the course of the very short 18 years when parents have the greatest influence, listening to children rather than talking to them is often the better choice. Certainly talking to (and sometimes even at!) our kids is important. In fact, most of us could probably spend a little more time doing just that. Despite the fact that God gave all of us two ears and only one mouth, it still seems to come more naturally for many of us to excessively use our one mouth, and to under-use our two ears.

There is another reason talking to our kids may often take priority over our listening to them. Child development experts tell us that it is important for parents of newborn infants and toddlers to expose them to words and language by talking to them as much as possible. In spite of the fact that they do not at first understand much of what Mom and Dad are saying, their consistently hearing words helps develop their vocabulary and verbal skills. This certainly is wise advice and is worthy of our following.

Early in their maturity, however, this need to hear words from us for the development of verbal skills is no longer as important as is their need to be heard and understood by us. It eventually becomes important for them to actually practice the verbal skills they have learned, and for us to become a sounding board or practice arena for them to express themselves and their ideas. It is easy for most of us to continue the pattern and practice of talking to (at) our kids when what they need more of is to be listened to and understood by us. So making the transition from talking to listening usually takes an intentional effort on our part.

## EARNING THE RIGHT TO BE HEARD

It is easy to ignore, dismiss, or minimize opportunities we have for conversation with our kids because the topic seems to be childish or insignificant. After all, we are important (or what we are doing is important) and time is valuable. We've got places to go and people to see! (Or T.V. to watch, chores to do, newspapers to read, or . . . ) But it is often the seemingly insignificant conversations that provide us with the opportunity to not only listen but to earn the right to be heard later on when our kids need to talk about something important.

Contrary to what many parents believe, being heard by our kids is not our birthright; we were not born with the right to be heard any more than we were born with the right to even be loved by them. It is not our right to be heard simply because we gave them life. Whether we like it or not, we must earn the right to be heard by our kids. While it must be earned, it is certainly reasonable and natural that we want to be heard by them. In fact, not only do we want to be heard, we **must** be heard by them as well.

Unfortunate as it may be, our kids were not born with a burning desire to listen to us or to take our advice. Their desire to hear what we have to say to them must be developed and earned by us. And it is ironic that our right to be heard and their desire to hear us are both earned primarily through our willingness to listen. The more our kids feel they have been heard and understood by us, the more willing they will be to listen to us when we do speak.

It is through listening now, to what might not be important or interesting, that we also increase the chances that someday they will come to us when they need to talk about issues that really do matter. On the other hand, if we do not listen to them when they are young, they will be far less likely to come to us later when they are dealing with serious, life changing questions. Like it or not, they are going to face issues that pose difficult questions for them to answer. Whether they are issues related to abortion, premarital sex, the existence of God, alcohol, choice of friends, or whether or not to go to college—they are sure to struggle with something. And by the time they do, we will have either earned the right to be heard, and they will look to us for advice and counsel, or they will exclude us from the process, convinced that because they were not heard before, they will not be heard now.

## WHAT'S A PARENT TO DO?

Suppose for a minute, that your little girl tells you that her dolly is sick. Do you take the time to listen and to express your concern, or do you ignore it or disregard it because you're busy? And besides, you're smart and you know that dolls don't get sick! Childhood fantasies like this one are normal and need to be taken seriously during the years when children are experimenting with imagination. Of course, if this kind of fantasy world continues into the teen years, you've got real problems!

Perhaps your son comes home and tells you that no one likes him at school. Do you dismiss his insecurity as typical for his age and in so doing, send the message that it shouldn't matter to him what others think of him? Rather than listening to his hurt, do you lecture him about how important it is for him to not care what others think? Or maybe you counter his expressed feelings of social insecurity by naming all the friends he has ever had. There is a place for all these efforts, but listening in such a way that conveys to him that you really understand and care that he is hurting is as beneficial to him as anything else you could say.

Imagine that you have just found evidence that leads you to suspect your daughter has lied about where she was on Friday night. Despite her futile efforts to get a word in edge-wise and declare she was where she said she was, you refuse to hear what she has to say (whether she is right or wrong, guilty or innocent isn't the point). Instead you launch into a lecture outlining her punishment and your disappointment, rather than listening to her side of the story. Your presumption of guilt has interfered with your willingness to listen.

Another possible way to handle this common teenage occurrence might go something like this:

"I have information that leads me to believe that you are not being completely truthful with me about where you've been. Do you have anything to say before I tell you what I've heard (or seen or observed, etc.)? I want to believe you but need to hear from you before I decide to believe you rather than the information I have. What do you have to say?"

Another example: You have just decided when your family will be taking the annual summer vacation and have announced the two-week time period to your kids. Rather than the excitement and gratitude you expected, you are told that the play-offs for your daughter's soccer league are right in the middle of the trip. To complicate matters further, your son has the opportunity to go to Europe during those same weeks with a friend's family. Since the dates you chose are the best for your schedule, you refuse to consider any ideas for a plan B that could possibly work for everyone.

A different response could communicate to your kids that you hear and understand what is important to them:

"Bummer. I was hoping that date would work well for everyone. I guess I should have checked with you before I made plans. Tell you what. Make sure the dates for your play- offs are definite, and double check what days you want to go to Europe, and I will see what other dates might work for my schedule. I can't promise anything, but I'd love to see you go to the finals with your team and it would be great for you to be able to go to Europe with your friend. I will see what I can do."

A family is not meant to run as a one-man, one-vote democracy. But it is important that our kids know they can be heard, and that they can in some way and to some degree, contribute to the decision-making process. Obviously, the degree of their influence will vary from situation to situation. They may under some circumstances be given an equal vote, while in other situations, just being able to state their opinion may be all they can expect.

## WHAT'S THE BOTTOM LINE?

Good and effective communication is made up of many different components. The one usually given the greatest importance is the ability to speak ideas, thoughts and emotions in a way that others are able to understand. As important as it is to be able to clearly speak our thoughts and ideas to our kids, it is equally important that we are able to listen to their thoughts and ideas.

We must earn the right to be heard and we do so primarily through time and effort spent listening to them. As much as we might wish it were not so, our right to be heard does not come naturally by virtue of our having given birth to them, nor simply because we are the parent. We must earn it.

Listening to our kids usually requires a great deal of time, discipline, and energy. And it might often be that we aren't interested in talking about the things they want to talk about. But in the long run, it is more likely that our greatest influence impact will come from having listened, rather than what we've said.

It seems more natural for most of us to want to talk more than we want to listen. But when we overcome that temptation and instead listen to our kids, we increase the probability that they will want to talk to us later on, and about things that really will matter.

What we have to say to our kids is certainly of great importance. But we will get their attention and earn the right to be heard not by talking, but by listening. And it is only then that we will be heard.

## DISCUSSION QUESTIONS:

1.  When you reflect on your childhood, do you recall whether or not your parents really listened to you?

2.  How did their listening (or not) affect you and your relationship with them?

3.  Do you agree or disagree with the suggestion that we must earn the right to be heard by our kids?

4.  When you are talking to your kids, do you feel that most of the time they are actually listening to what you have to say?

5.  Do you really listen to your kids when they talk or are you more eager to get your own thoughts across to them?

6.  What physical signs from you do your kids see that show them they are being heard?

*"When we consistently protect our kids from learning through their mistakes and the consequences that may follow, we rob them of independence and self-reliance."*

# Question #18:

## *Do I allow my kids as many choices as possible?*

GIVING OUR YOUNG KIDS CHOICES rather than making decisions for them, is not an inclination that comes easily for any of us parents. And although most of us do realize the importance of gradually turning over the reins of control to them, it usually takes a bit of will power and discipline on our part to follow through with our commitment to do so. While there may be many reasons why it is difficult for most of us to encourage our kids to choose and decide for themselves, two are most common:

First, it is usually much easier and quicker for us to make decisions ourselves and then to follow through with what we have decided, than it is to walk our kids through the learning process of decision-making. Out of necessity, we exhausted parents are usually looking for quicker and easier ways of doing things. So it is a natural temptation in our busy lives to simply make choices and decisions for them, even when they are capable of learning to make them for themselves.

Although it takes more time and energy to offer our kids choices and to encourage their decision-making skills, it is important that our efforts to do so begin early in their lives. What weary parent would disagree that it is far easier to pick out what their 1st grader will wear to school the next day, than it is to pick out three outfits and then allow them to decide which they would like to wear? It is much easier and far less time consuming to give in to the temptation of making the choice ourselves, rather than taking the time and effort to explain what options they have and why.

The second reason for the reluctance in some parents to gradually encourage their kids to make their own decisions and choices is perhaps the most common. Giving them the freedom to choose and decide for themselves requires that we risk the possibility of their being affected negatively in some way as a result. And to make letting go even more difficult, we must face the possibility that the choices they make may not be what we would make for them if it were up to us. As every parent that has taken this risk knows, there will be mistakes made—and consequences to be paid as a result—that could have been avoided if only we had made the decision for them.

Examples of this reluctance to gradually turn control over to their children can be seen as they grow into young adults and move on to college. Recently, many colleges have established the rule that no parent be present with their student during the registration process. Apparently this has become necessary since academic choices are more and more commonly made by parents rather than by the students themselves. As a result, many students have been discouraged from seeking their own academic and professional path. Some schools have even taken the further step of banning cell phones from the registration setting because—in an effort to side-step the parental ban—phone calls for direction and decision-making have become common place.

## GIVING KIDS THE FREEDOM TO MAKE DECISIONS AND CHOICES, WITHIN GUIDELINES

Because there are many risks involved in this process of learning the fine art of decision-making, it is important that we provide our kids with guidelines and boundaries within which they can either succeed or safely fail. And as they improve in their ability to make good choices, our guidelines for their decision-making may then gradually be expanded, allowing them more room for independence. It is the presence of guidelines that limit the degree and severity of consequences that may result due to any possible error in judgment. As we allow and encourage them to make choices and decisions for themselves, we gradually give up our control over them.

## Giving kids choices teaches cause and affect thinking

Even though they run the risk of making mistakes, there are a number of reasons it is important to allow our kids the freedom to make choices. For starters, kids who are not encouraged to make decisions within healthy and appropriate guidelines are deprived of learning "cause and affect" reasoning. This "if-then" thinking process is at the heart of all good decision-making, and it is a process that is learned through the experience of trial and error. When children are given guidelines and boundaries within which they can safely risk making choices and decisions, they are given the tools to help them master the all important cause and effect decision-making process. Some of their choices will be good ones and will help create self-confidence; others will not be the best, and they will learn as a result what went wrong, how to avoid the same mistake next time. With our help, they will likely improve and fine-tune their decision-making skills and continually learn how to make better decisions.

It is interesting that when highly successful people are asked to talk about their journey toward success, they will often refer to and emphasize the failures they experienced along the way. Most will talk about how their failures became stepping stones toward achieving the goals they had set for themselves. In other words, most people who have achieved a high-level of success report that they did so as a result of experiencing and then understanding their failures. Our kids will also learn to succeed by going through and understanding their failures and it is our responsibility to provide them with both a reasonable amount of safety, and at the same time, the freedom to learn by way of trial and error.

We all want as much control in and over our own lives as possible, and there are many areas of living where we do not have as much control as we would like. Our kids are no different. Those who grow up feeling confident in their ability to make good decisions experience a greater degree of this desired control in and over their lives. The security of being in control comes from knowing how to evaluate cause and effect decisions: "If I do this, then I can likely count on this." When kids have not learned to use this all important "if-then" reasoning, they will lack a sense of healthy control in their lives.

## ENCOURAGES SELF-RELIANCE

Learning to make wise and successful decisions helps our kids develop self-reliance, individuality, and independence. If, on the other hand, they learn to rely on you to make decisions for them, then it is more likely that they will grow up to be teenagers—eventually adults—who continue to look to others to guide and direct life for them. It is not difficult to see the potential danger of such dependence upon others.

## DEVELOPS SELF CONFIDENCE

Self confidence is another facet of development that is affected— one way or another—by their ability to make healthy choices for themselves. The feeling of greater control and appropriate self-reliance helps feed their sense of feeling safe. On the other hand, kids who grow up needing and expecting others to make decisions for them, rather than choosing for themselves, usually do not feel as secure about who they are and what they have to offer in life.

## WHAT'S A PARENT TO DO?

So practically speaking, just what does this process of teaching and encouraging our kids the fine art of making healthy choices look like? Clearly, setting and communicating our guidelines is the first step. Then it is important to state specifically what the options are that they have to consider and to choose from. A general rule of thumb is that the younger they are, the fewer possibilities they should be given from which to choose. Too many options for younger kids can be overwhelming, while too few for older ones can be excessively limiting.

"It's going to be cold today so you may wear any of your long-sleeved shirts. Which one you wear is up to you."

"You may have a friend over either Friday or Saturday night. But remember that you have to get up early Sunday morning for church. So Friday might be best. It's your choice, so which ever you decide is ok with me."

"You have $5 to spend this week. It's up to you how you spend it, but when you're in the video store tomorrow, remember that if you spend it all there, you will be broke for the rest of the week."

"Your mom and I think that you have been on the go far too much so this weekend. You may go out either Friday night, or you can be out Saturday. Which you choose is up to you."

## WHAT'S THE BOTTOM LINE?

It is usually easier for us to make choices for our kids rather than to take the risk of turning the reins of control over to them. But if we do not give them choices to make for themselves, then we run the risk of interfering with their developing the independence that will be important for them to have after they are no longer in our care. Encouraging them in their decision-making process, along with allowing them to safely learn through trial and error will go a long way in helping them develop a spirit of independence. When we "short circuit" that process by making decisions for them, we deprive them of what can be learned through the decision-making process. It is often a slower, more tedious effort for us, but one that will pay off in the long run.

Boundaries—guidelines within which children may freely function—are important. And ideally, as our kids grow and mature, the guidelines we establish will grow wider, giving them more freedom to choose and to make their own decisions. Eventually, the guidelines we have set for them will be completely replaced by guidelines they have established for themselves. Boundaries never go away; they just get transferred from being ours, to being theirs (and society's) as they grow and mature into adulthood.

Giving our kids as many choices in life as possible does not mean that we must always allow them to choose for themselves. As kids struggle through life's obstacles and attempt to find and establish their independence, they are often motivated by what feels good immediately, rather than by what is right or best for them in the long run. So our guidance in the form of boundaries, within which they can choose and decide for themselves, is essential for their safety; sometimes, the possible negative consequences are simply too great to support a "just let them choose for themselves and they can learn the hard way" philosophy.

There are times when we must significantly narrow the boundaries within which they are free to choose by resorting to a firm, benevolent, dictatorial, "No." As a general rule though, our goal must be to allow them as much freedom as possible at all stages of their lives. As they are given this freedom, they will learn to choose, decide, and develop safely by thinking through the "if-then," and "cause and effect" learning experiences of life.

It is often true that letting them learn the "hard way" (as long as it is not *too* hard) is actually the best way for our kids to learn. When we constantly protect them from learning from their mistakes and the consequences that result, we may interfere with their developing independence and self-reliance. Once again, we parents are faced with a judgment call that is not always easy to make.

Raising healthy and responsible kids requires that we allow them the freedom necessary to develop an independent and self-reliant spirit. Like all other areas of successful parenting, perfection is not required. There is room for some error on our part and we can still be successful parents, even if we don't always get it right. Our goal must be to remember that it is important to give our children as many choices in life as possible. Doing it correctly every time is simply not required.

## Discussion Questions:

1. Did your parents encourage you to make choices and decisions when you were growing up?

2. Did you usually feel safe in making those choices, or were you often left on your own to make decisions you were not mature enough to safely make?

3. As a parent today do you encourage your kids to choose for themselves when it is appropriate and safe to do so?

4. What are some results of encouraging (or not) your kids to make decisions and choices for themselves?

5. How do you tend to respond when you give them freedom to choose, and they make choices you do not agree with?

6. Are there some areas in which you are willing to give your kids more choices?

7. Do you have any fears of giving them more freedom to choose and to decide for themselves?

"*Establishing boundaries within which our kids may freely function is essential if they are to effectively consider the consequences of their behavior.*"

# Question #19:

## *Do I establish appropriate boundaries and guidelines in which my kids may freely and safely function?*

THE PREVIOUS CHAPTER ADDRESSED the importance of establishing guidelines and boundaries for the purpose of giving your kids as much safety as possible while learning to make successful choices and decisions. In this chapter we are once again addressing the importance of establishing guidelines and boundaries, but for reasons that go beyond their need for safety.

Another responsibility we parents have (as if we needed another one!) is to establish reasonable rules, and expectations for the behavior and conduct of our children. We do this best by not only establishing boundaries and guidelines, but by communicating to them what our expectations are and what consequences they can expect when they step outside those boundaries. As we accomplish this, we gradually prepare them for a world that is full of expectations, as well as consequences for unacceptable behaviors. This is just one of the many life lessons that must be learned early in their lives and through their relationship with their parents.

Without reasonable expectations to guide our conduct and behaviors, our world would be an even less civilized place than it already is. So it is true, for all of us, that having guidelines and parameters in which we are then able to freely live is necessary to our health and well-being. Clear and fair guidelines, expectations and consequences provide us all with as much predictability as possible, and as a result we are able to go about our lives with a high degree of the safety and security that is essential for living healthy and productive lives. Without guidelines, boundaries and reasonable expectations to live by, our world would be without order.

We have all had the experience of driving down the freeway at night when suddenly the road changes from rugged, worn, somewhat bumpy and kind of grey, to smooth as silk and black as coal. With little warning, the lines that had been there just moments before disappear and are no longer present to restrict us. At first we kind of enjoy our new found freedom to drive wherever on the road's surface we please. But then we realize that those familiar lines which limited us are no longer there to guide us either.

Gone too are the little reflective bumps that just seconds ago were in the middle of the road and along the edge. They are no longer an irritant to us when we occasionally "get out of line" and run over them, but we are also no longer able to rely on them to tell us where we belong or what's expected of us. We no longer have the benefit of those reflective bumps in our road that—while at times irritating—served us well by showing us what was expected of us, as well as what we could count on from others.

It quickly becomes apparent that a highway crew has recently resurfaced the road but has not yet returned to repaint the stripes or replace the little plastic reflector bumps. To make matters worse, our anxieties and insecurities increase as we realize that the oncoming traffic has no lines either. And the people in those approaching cars don't know any better than we do exactly where they belong and what is expected of them!

We are on our own, at least for the moment. And in spite of the greater freedom we now have due to the absence of guidelines, we really don't like it at all! We don't like it because we want and need to know what to expect from others and what is expected and required of us. In losing this structure of clear and well-defined expectations for how we are to conduct ourselves, we have also lost the feeling of security and predictability that is important if we are to feel safe and secure.

It is no different for our kids.

At last, and none too soon, the lines reappear and again we know what is expected of us. And just as importantly, we again know what to expect from the on-coming traffic. We feel safe and more secure because we have again been given expectations for our conduct and behavior, along with restrictions that are good for us as well. We are free once again—within clearly defined limitations—to move about freely and as we please.

## THE IMPORTANCE OF PREDICTABILITY

One of the reasons we are all at best "normal neurotics" is that none of us can fully predict what is going to happen next in life. It is this uncertainty that creates some degree of anxiety in all of us. So when we provide our kids with freedom within guidelines, expectations and consequences, we help provide some degree of predictability that will benefit them on the road they travel in life.

While they may not always like or value the limitations and restrictions we place on them, when we do not, they become insecure and unsure. When appropriate and consistent guidelines and expectations are in place and they are allowed to then freely function within them, they enjoy a greater degree of predictability which is essential if they are to grow up healthy and well-adjusted.

An unfortunate pattern in our society is the failure of many families to successfully teach the clear, consistent "cause and effect" reasoning that helps develop a greater degree of predictability. "If I do . . . such and such, then the likely result will be . . . such and such. Therefore, I'd better not do it." Evidence to support the notion that many individuals in our world lack the ability to consider the consequences of their actions can be found in any corner newsstand.

## BOUNDARIES, EXPECTATIONS AND CONSEQUENCES CAN BE TOO RESTRICTIVE

Remember that our kids are in the process of becoming, and that it is through trial and error that they learn a great deal about themselves and their world. It is a temptation for many parents to establish guidelines and parameters for their kids that are too narrow and limiting, excessively restricting them. When the guidelines and boundaries are unrealistically narrow and restrictive, kids will be limited in their ability to safely test, explore, and to learn.

What often results when guidelines and expectations are consistently and excessively narrow and restrictive is one of two broad but opposite life patterns: Kids may either give up and assume a what's-the-use attitude and passively stand by while life happens to them. Or they may respond in the opposite direction by attempting to break out of their excessively restrictive guidelines in dangerous and destructive ways. That's what we in the trade call destructive and self-defeating rebellion! Neither is a healthy or desired alternative.

## BOUNDARIES, EXPECTATIONS AND CONSEQUENCES CAN BE TOO PERMISSIVE

When guidelines and boundaries are excessively permissive and without reasonable expectations, other difficulties may arise. When our boundaries are too broad, children have only a few of the standards and expectations that are needed for them to safely experiment, discover, and to learn. When we provide little of the safety that is needed for them to fail and then to learn from those failures, we put them in a position of making choices and decisions they are not yet ready or prepared to make. By doing so we set them up to fail, with very little to gain or to learn from their failures.

The outcome from excessively permissive boundaries and guidelines may result in the negative long-term rebellious behavior of reacting without good and proper judgment. This type of rebellion seems to beg for the safety of guidelines within which to live. Their reaction to the absence of standards and expectations is often a cry for help in the form of unhealthy and destructive rebellion. It must feel something similar to how we felt back on our repaved road when the guidelines were no longer present to guide us, to restrict us, and to keep us safe.

## What's a parent to do?

While we must wisely establish boundaries, guidelines and expectations that are not too broad, and at the same time not too narrow, it is equally important that we know how far to adjust them, and when it is appropriate to do so. A number of variables enter the picture when we consider changing or adjusting our boundaries and expectations. For example, our kids may demonstrate through their increasingly responsible attitudes and behaviors that they are able to handle a situation we might have previously believed they weren't ready for. With age often comes a natural widening of the guidelines, but their actions must also show that giving them more freedom is justified.

"You know Kelly, we set your curfew at midnight about 6 months ago and I have to say we have been very pleased that you have done so well at living by the hours we set for you. We know it hasn't always been easy, and you haven't always been happy with your hours since many of your friends don't have to be in until 1 a.m. Since you have done so well cooperating with us—even being home early at times—we want to extend your curfew to 1 a.m. if whatever you have planned warrants it. Just let us know when you need a little more time, tell us what you have planned, and you can count on a little more wiggle room from us. Thanks for being so cooperative."

It may sometimes be appropriate to "bargain" with your kids when they try to convince us that they can handle broader boundaries. From time to time, consider making a deal with them that if they abide by certain conditions, you will give them a little more freedom. Parents must also be willing to learn by safe trial and error in an effort to set healthy and appropriate guidelines for ever-growing, ever-changing kids. There are many other events and circumstances that will help evaluate when it is time to readjust the boundaries we have previously established. Ultimately, it is important that you keep an open mind to the possibility of giving your kids more and more freedom to experiment.

"Casey, you've been asking for some time now to have friends sleep over on Friday nights. We have always held firm to not allowing that because you have to be up so early for practice every Saturday morning. We still aren't all together sure it's a good idea, but you are almost 15 and maybe you should be making more of these decisions for yourself. So we are willing to make you a deal. We will agree to letting you choose no more than two Friday nights per month to have a friend sleep over, but only as long as you are up in plenty of time to make practice. We all know that when you haven't had enough sleep, your studies can suffer and, well, you know you can be a bit of a grump too. So we will agree to more freedom as long as you keep up your studies and your mood around here doesn't make life hard for the rest of us. Then, we will evaluate with you in a couple of months and decide to either go back to the original rule of no Friday night sleepovers, keep it the same for awhile longer, or maybe to even give you freedom for more Friday night guests. Is it a deal?"

It may be a difficult concept for us to accept, but our kids really do have choices to make about staying within our boundaries and expectations. They do have the freedom of choosing to obey or to disobey, so it is important that you clearly communicate what the consequences of their choices and actions will be. This predictability enables them to process their decision through "if-then" reasoning. In this way, they are more able to determine what their actions will cost them, and whether or not the fun, high, or whatever it is that the disobedience gives them, is worth the consequences they will face as a result. Hopefully, they'll choose correctly most of the time!

"In spite of the fact that your mom and I have to unexpectedly be gone Friday night and Saturday, your week-end grounding from yesterday's incident remains in force. Corey, we understand that you could decide to disregard your grounding while we are gone, but we trust you to abide by the expectations we have of you. However, if you choose to defy us, you will face the greater consequences of much longer grounding. We really hope you'll abide by the rules while we are gone."

## WHAT'S THE BOTTOM LINE?

Our kids must know as clearly as possible what the boundaries are in which they can freely live their lives. It is equally important that you teach them how to process their decisions in terms of "cause and effect" outcomes. Knowing the consequences of their behavior is another way you can help prepare them for life outside of their relationship with you.

Since there will always be authority figures to comply with in their lives, being able to evaluate expectations and consequences is a skill essential to living a healthy adult life. While authority is certainly not always correct, it does provide a necessary structure for living civil and decent lives in a very crowded and untamed world.

Raising healthy and well-adjusted kids requires that we parents provide guidelines that create a safe environment within which our kids can learn through testing. It is only within the safety of our boundaries and expectations that kids will take healthy and appropriate risks, and learn through trial and error behavior.

Establishing guidelines within which our kids may freely "move around" requires that we be specific about what we expect, and then equally specific and consistent about the consequences they can count on if they step outside our established boundaries. Knowing ahead of time (predictability) strengthens their ability to think, consider, and to process in terms of that all important "cause and effect" reasoning.

## DISCUSSION QUESTIONS:

1.  Looking back on your childhood, do you believe that your parents usually established boundaries and expectations that were too broad, too narrow, or just right?

2.  Were you free to function basically on your own, but within safe and predictable boundaries and guidelines?

3.  How did the guidelines your parents established for you as a child shape you as you grew and matured?

4.  On what do you base your decisions regarding the guidelines and expectations you establish for your kids (maturity, what others might think, age, past ability to handle freedom, etc.)?

5.  Generally, how well are your kids doing within the boundaries and expectations you have established for them?

6.  How well do you think you do with establishing guidelines and expectations within which your kids can freely function?

"Our love and acceptance is not a tool for persuading our kids to behave or to live up to our expectations."

# Question #20:

*When my kids disappoint me, do I require that they earn back my love and acceptance?*

MOST OF US HAVE BEEN in a relationship or two where we have disappointed, or in some way let another person down. It may even be that we lost their respect, affection, and acceptance as a result of something we had done or said. It might have been a boss or supervisor who was disappointed in our work performance or it might have been our spouse who was let down by our attitude or behavior. It might have been a close friend who pulled away from us, sending the message that we had some serious work to do in order to regain their love and affection.

Whether it was a friend, parent, boss, co-worker, or even one of our own kids who seemed to only love and accept us conditionally, most of us have felt a cold distance come between ourselves and someone we cared for. As a result of our own experience with conditional love or acceptance, most of us can relate to just how badly rejection and withdrawal can feel, even when it is temporary.

It is certain that when our kids disappoint us, hurt us, make us mad, or let us down in any other way (and they will!), our response to them will send a strong and significant message. And that message is sure to either have a positive influence, or it will affect them in a negative way. How we respond when they have disappointed will either convey to them how very much we love and value them in spite of our disappointment, hurt or general disapproval, or it will send the very different message that they must now work very hard to earn back our love and approval.

When we consistently respond to the mistakes and errors that our kids make by attaching strings to our love and affection for them, they will likely conclude that if they are to be accepted and valued by others, that it is necessary to live up to the expectations and desires of the people around them. If our kids conclude that our love and acceptance for them is based on how they behave, how they perform or how they live up to our expectations of them, does it not stand to reason that they will be more likely to carry that conclusion into their relationships with others? So when you offer strings-attached love and acceptance to your kids, you risk the possibility of their learning to place an excessive amount of importance on what others think of them as well.

The need to please others and to be accepted by them are not necessarily unhealthy needs, but when those needs becomes a primary motivation for behavior, then life becomes an ongoing process of wearing the "right mask" at the "right time" for the "right person." When this masquerade becomes a life pattern, the need for acceptance becomes a primary motivating factor, thus hindering the authentic self. When kids learn to wear masks in an effort to gain approval and love, over time they are more likely to lose track of who they really are and instead, become shaped and disguised by what others expect them to be.

## DISAPPROVAL WITHOUT DISGUST

Does this mean then that we must never disapprove of unacceptable behaviors or attitudes? Is this to suggest that we parents must never challenge or attempt to correct our children? Are we to be outwardly approving of their behaviors even though we privately disapprove? Should we never send them to their room for misbehaving for fear of their feeling rejected? Certainly not, to all of these questions!

A parent's kind but firm corrections are a major shaping force in their learning what is right and what is wrong, what is acceptable, and what is not. And it is our responsibility, as parents who strive to raise healthy kids, to challenge, correct and to shape them in order to help develop within them a healthy conscience. In order to do this, we must at times show and express our disapproval, but without withdrawing from them; we must at times be appropriately angry, without the rejection and disgust that can easily accompany correction.

Someone once shared with me a childhood memory that relates to keeping kids accountable while loving them unconditionally. This man's mother was a religious woman with a strong belief in God's unconditional love for her. When she disciplined her son, she would usually add to whatever the consequences were for the particular misbehavior, "Remember, God and I know all there is to know about you and we love you anyway!" This assurance of her love was almost always given with a big hug, a twinkle in her eye and a smile on her face that reminded him that once again her love was unconditional. According to this fortunate man, he always knew where he stood with his mom (and with his God) since she constantly assured him that there were no conditions placed upon her love and acceptance of him.

## WHAT'S A PARENT TO DO?

Consider the following possible responses from a parent who has just discovered that their son has been stealing money from them. It is clear which one sends the message that he must somehow perform in order to regain his parent's acceptance, and which one is the healthy and corrective response that is meant (in no uncertain terms!) to bring about changes in behaviors while leaving love and acceptance clearly in place.

"I've always wondered if you were an honest person. Maybe when you've proven to me that you are, I will be able to forgive you." vs. "Your actions are not consistent with the kind of person I know you are. We need to talk about why you did this."

"In case you've been wondering why I haven't been speaking to you the last several days, I am waiting for you to show me that this stealing will never happen again." vs. "I am very disappointed in you, and to tell you the truth, I'm angry as well. But regardless of what you've done, I want you to know that I love you anyway. What do you think your consequences should be, and what do you think can be done to prevent this from happening again? Let's talk about it once we've had some time to think about what has happened."

"I've wondered lately if you could be trusted. Now that you have shown me that you can't be, don't expect me to give you the benefit of the doubt any longer." vs. "You are better than this, and stealing is just not like you. Let's work together to understand why you did it, and what should be done to prevent it from happening again".

There are good and effective ways of saying to our kids that we want them to go away and think about what just happened without rejecting and discounting them. Of course, there are also ways of responding that are destructive and not a part of productive parenting. Consider the differences in the following responses:

"I've been putting up with your moaning and groaning long enough Carrie. Go to your room and I will let you know when you can come out." (Two hours later, the detention is over but it is not followed with conversation about what happened and what can be learned. Instead, there is silence and distance that says Mom or Dad are still not over it).

Or, "I've quietly waited, Carrie, for over five minutes now for you to change the tone of your voice and attitude. Instead, both are getting more difficult for the rest of us to be around. I want you to go to your room. You may be in there for thirty seconds, or you may choose to be there the rest of the afternoon and into the evening. When it is time for you to come out is completely up to you, but make sure that you do not come out before you have decided you can act and behave in a way that doesn't negatively affect the rest of us. Personally, I hope you decide you can come out real soon because I'd like to be with you. But stay in your room until you are ready to adjust your behaviors because next time I will decide how long you need to be in your room, and you might not like how long I will ask you to stay there." (We aren't sure how long Carrie stayed in her room but when she did come out, Mom smiled approvingly and said she was glad she was back to her good and enjoyable self.)

## What's the bottom line?

Remember from Chapter 1—"What do my kids hear me say about them?"—that your kids have a developing brain that is like a sponge that absorbs what it observes and what it is told. During their early years of development, they will learn to either live up to, or they will live down, the messages about themselves that they consistently hear from you. And then, beyond their years with you, they will likely set out in life to continue on that path that was established early on. If they conclude, having experienced conditional love, that they are more "leaveable" than they are loveable, they will move on in life concluding the same in their relationships with others.

Along with all the other important responsibilities that go along with being a parent, is the task of showing them that there is nothing they could do to cause you to physically or emotionally withdraw your love and acceptance of them. You must show them through your responses, even when you have in some way been hurt or disappointed by them, that there is simply no way they will ever succeed at pushing you away.

Kids can disappoint us, they can frustrate us, they can rebel and they can even make us angry or bring us to tears. They are even capable of pushing us to the brink of despair, but they can never push away.

It is essential that we give our kids a clear message of disapproval when they challenge, misbehave, disobey or in any other way step outside the boundaries we have established. But rather than our disappointment, hurt and anger, we must in the midst of our discipline, use the influence of our love and acceptance as a tool to encourage and to gain their cooperation and compliance with our authority in their lives.

## DISCUSSION QUESTIONS:

1.  Did your parents have "no strings attached" love toward you, even when you misbehaved or disappointed them in some way?

2.  How did their attitude about accepting and loving you either conditionally or unconditionally affect your growing up?

3.  Does the attitude they had toward you then continue to affect you in any way today?

4.  How would you rate or evaluate your ability to show your love in the midst of their disappointing or disobeying you?

5.  From what you are able to observe, do your kids seem to think that they must somehow earn peer acceptance by living up (or down) to the expectations that are placed on them?

6.  What are some ways you can communicate disapproval without disgust or rejection?

"When we parents fail to recognize and accept that challenges to our authority are normal and even necessary for our kids to learn how to think for themselves, we run the risk of responding to their challenges in ways that may actually lead to the unnecessary and destructive rebellion we'd all like to avoid."

## Question #21:

*Do I recognize that it is normal for my kids to challenge my authority?*

ONE OF THE MANY changes our kids must go through, as they mature, is transitioning from, "If they say so, it must be true," to "Wait a minute. What do I think?" Helping them in this difficult transition is another responsibility we parents must take on if our kids are to gradually learn to think, evaluate, and to make their own decisions. Our goal is not to bring them to a point where they no longer need or welcome input from us or others at all, but we do want them to learn to make decisions for themselves rather than to rely on others to think and to decide for them.

### RECOGNIZING THE DIFFERENCE BETWEEN A CHALLENGE AND REBELLION

It is essential to understand the differences between a child who is challenging your authority, and a child who is rebelling, in an attempt to undermine our authority. Each is powered by different motivations and it is important that we spot the differences and respond appropriately.

Challenges to our authority are inevitable and even necessary if our kids are to grow and mature. Rebellion, on the other hand, is not (at least as a consistent pattern) inevitable or necessary, and is seldom helpful to the growth process and development of our kids. While most parents, and kids alike, do survive it, rebellion is destructive and the cost of any lessons learned is usually high.

A common mistake that many parents make, which can lead to the needless and destructive rebellion that occurs in kids these days, is this:

> When we parents fail to understand and accept that challenges to our authority are normal and even necessary for our kids to learn how to think for themselves, we run the risk of responding to their challenges in ways that may actually lead to the unnecessary and destructive rebellion we'd all like to avoid.

Challenges to our authority provide opportunities for learning, for teaching, and for opportunities to help our kids to grow and mature. It can even be argued that without their challenges and our appropriate responses to them, that it would be difficult for them to learn the fine art of thinking for themselves. Most challenges to our authority are over common issues like pressure from peers ("But *everyone* is doing it!), limitations we place on them that they don't like, or expectations we have of them that they may think are unfair. And at some point, good old fashioned hormones kick in and may also play a part in their challenging our role as an authority in their lives. How we respond to the inevitable challenges that are part of their development and maturity will either help us avoid destructive and needless rebellion, or provoke them in such a way that sets the stage for destructive rebellion. When we incorrectly assume that their challenging us is motivated by a desire to usurp our authority, we run the risk of overreacting and responding in a way that encourages their rebellion.

## RECOGNIZING THE DIFFERENCE BETWEEN THEIR SPIRIT AND THEIR WILL

While it is essential that we distinguish between their necessary and inevitable challenges of us, and their attempts to rebel in order to undermine our authority, it is of equal importance that we understand the distinctions between their spirit, and their will. It is easy to confuse the will and the spirit, and to use simply use the terms interchangeably. But in fact, they are two very different facets of a child's makeup.

## THE SPIRIT

The spirit refers to the attitudes we develop about ourselves as well as toward life in general. A healthy spirit reflects an attitude of self acceptance and a well-balanced and realistic assessment of one's worth and value. A healthy spirit is also reflective of a person who has enthusiasm, energy, and excitement for living life. All of this we must help preserve and encourage in our kids.

## THE WILL

The will refers to what is a natural tendency to be defiant, self-centered and demanding. While it is a debatable issue, I suspect that as human beings, a strong will (i.e., our bent toward a selfish and demanding attitude) is innate. But whether we are born with this tendency or we develop it after birth, it must be in all of us be shaped and controlled if we are to learn the importance of taking into consideration the needs and desires of others.

When we mistake healthy and necessary challenges to our authority, for defiant rebellion, and then react as if they were attempts to undermine our authority, we run the risk of stifling their spirit and at the same time, enflaming the defiant will. Our goal must be the opposite; we must encourage their spirit and stifle defiant will.

## WHY DO THEY CHALLENGE MY AUTHORITY, AND DO I HAVE TO LIKE IT?

Once again, it may be helpful to review Chapter 1 (What do my kids hear me say about them?) which addresses how young kids have not yet fully developed the ability to think or reason for themselves. Their brain capacity, which is necessary for independent thinking and reasoning, grows and expands over a period of time and as a result of life experience.

Since their brains in some ways function more like a sponge than a fully developed adult brain, they are not yet able to think for themselves. Instead, at first they are only capable of taking what they hear and see from us, (as well as what they hear and observe from others around them) and absorbing that information as truth. Not only do they absorb without question what they hear us say about them, but also what they hear us say about lots of other things as well. Our task as their parents is to help take them from that early stage of blind acceptance, to the ability to reason on their own.

This is certainly a good and honorable goal for us to have for our kids. What parent would not want their kids to develop an ability and desire to think for themselves, as opposed to forever handing over such incredible power and influence to others? But as they grow older and begin to develop the ability to question and to make their own decisions, it is natural and understandable that we may begin resisting their practicing on us as a way of making this transition. Why can't they just continue taking our word for everything and then when they turn 18 and leave home, maybe then they can start thinking for themselves! Now there's an idea most of us parents could get behind! If only it worked that way.

As difficult as it is for most of us when our kids begin to challenge our authority (especially when we remember back on the warm and close relationship we once had with them when they didn't really question us), how could it be any other way? If it is our goal to take this "unfinished product" who has always accepted as truth anything and everything they heard from others around them, and to help them develop the capacity to think for themselves, then even though we won't always like it, they must first learn to question and to think independently within the safety of their relationship with us. This transition into independent thinking is where challenging you—in some form and to some degree or another—enters the picture.

As kids begin to think for themselves, and to try out their new found reasoning skills, it is natural for most parents to fear losing their influence: "How can they challenge and question me? I've always been their hero!" This new phase is usually met with mixed and conflicting emotions. On one hand, we really do want them to eventually be wise and independent thinkers, but when they practice their new assertiveness, it does not always sit well.

When they begin for the first time to question our word, our authority and how we view things, it is easily mistaken as unacceptable rebellion. Although their new behaviors and attitudes may pose a threat to our role in their lives, their motivations may not be what typically lead to unacceptable rebellion. Instead, they may be challenging our authority in a way that is necessary in the process of learning to think and to reason for themselves. It is kind of ironic, isn't it, that while we want them to think and reason for themselves, we want them to practice on others rather than on us.

So like it or not, (and it is understandable not to like it at times!) somewhere in the process of their learning and growing, they stop letting us think for them and they begin to challenge us. This change from our having been the expert and the hero in their eyes on just about everything, to somehow always being wrong and seemingly knowing absolutely nothing, may happen gradually and over a period of time, or it may seem to show up overnight, out of nowhere, and for no apparent reason.

## LOOK HOW YOU MAKE ME LOOK!

Another reason it may be difficult for some of us to allow and encourage our kids to think for themselves is that most of us are proud and have egos. And naturally our egos are to some degree connected to the successes and failures as parents. While this is normal and understandable, our need to look good—not only in the eyes of others, but in our own eyes as well—can interfere with our willingness to be challenged by our kids.

Of course it is reasonable and understandable that we want to perceive ourselves—as well as be seen by others—as a good and successful parent. But the desire to look good can lead to a, "look how you make me look as your parent," attitude. For some, ego will not allow them to accept the necessity of their kids learning to think for themselves for fear of how it will reflect on them.

The truth is that the behaviors and attitudes of our children, as well as the decisions they make, can indeed be a reflection on us as parents. As our kids learn to think for themselves, they have the ability to make us look good in the eyes of others, or they can make us look bad. But when our responses to them are motivated by how we might be seen and thought of when they challenge and insist on thinking for themselves, then what may start out as normal and even necessary challenges to our authority can become full-blown and destructive rebellion.

## WHAT'S A PARENT TO DO?

Remember that challenges to your authority are normal—even necessary—for your kids to develop the ability to think for themselves. When they challenge your authority, be careful to respond in ways that do not damage their spirit. Avoid making your responses a personal attack on them.

Avoid withdrawing from them because they have challenged or questioned you. Withdrawing or rejecting damages their spirit and at the same time, encourages willful defiance.

When you children disagree with you in ways that challenge your authority, resist the temptation of refusing to talk or listen to them. When you refuse to communicate because you have been challenged, you damage their spirit rather than addressing their will. Refusing to communicate increases the chances that they will rebel in destructive and unhealthy ways.

Avoid using guilt to defend against challenges to your authority. Guilt attacks their spirit rather than their willfulness and it sets the stage for rebellion.

Let them know that as long as they respect that you are the final authority, that it is ok for them to verbally question you about the decisions that affect them. This too, is easier said than done since most of us do not like the idea of being questioned by our kids. However, doing so opens up communication and allows them to be genuinely heard in a way that will help discourage the need to rebel.

Regularly ask your kids what they think about various ideas and issues. Consistently let them know that it is ok if their opinions are different than yours. Remind them that it is important that they develop an ability to think for themselves even if what they conclude conflicts with you and what your opinions are.

## WHAT'S THE BOTTOM LINE?

Challenges to a parents' authority are normal and even necessary. When we remember this we are less likely to take them as a personal assault on our authority, and will be more likely to avoid reacting in ways that lead to and encourage rebellion.

When we accept the fact that it is normal and necessary for our kids to go through a phase of challenging us, we are more likely to successfully place ourselves on the same side as them, rather than being seen as the enemy. This enables you to work together toward a common goal, rather than competing against them in a tug-of-war where someone has to lose. Rather than being seen as the "enemy to defeat" you will more likely (at least eventually) become a trusted advocate with whom they want to work.

Understanding and accepting that challenges to your authority are normal is yet another one of those parenting skills that is easier said than done and it seldom works quite as smoothly as all that is suggested here makes it sound. But it is possible to survive and to even thrive in this inevitable stage where your authority begins to be challenged.

None of these ideas regarding appropriate challenges and destructive rebellion are meant to suggest that if our kids resort to unhealthy and destructive rebellion, it is necessarily because we have confused their necessary challenges with their attempting to undermine our authority. We are all affected and shaped more by how we choose to respond to the treatment we have received from others, and less by the actual treatment we received. We must all take responsibility for how we respond, and our kids are no exception. It is nonetheless important to consider how our responses and interactions toward them can either discourage or encourage unhealthy, destructive rebellion as they are learning to think independently and for themselves.

## DISCUSSION QUESTIONS:

1. How did your parents deal with your challenges to their authority?

2. Were their responses helpful and constructive, or did their reactions lead to destructive rebellion in you?

3. Do you agree/disagree with the idea that challenges to your authority is not only inevitable, but necessary in their developing independence?

4. How do you usually respond when your kids challenge your authority?

5. When your kids challenge your authority, do you use guilt, condemnation, or perhaps shame to get them to submit or shape-up?

6. Do you sometimes take their challenges personally ("look how you make me look!")?

7. What are some alternative ways of dealing with your kids and their inevitable challenges to your authority?

# Conclusion

SO THERE YOU HAVE it. Everything you ever wanted to know about raising healthy and well-adjusted kids—and all in one simple little book! If only being a parent were that easy.

Considering these 21 questions merely scratches the surface of what is required for being a successful parent. There is so much more to understand about this difficult but exciting and rewarding adventure called parenting. And as is usually the case, understanding what must be done is the easy part. The real work now lies ahead and will take discipline, determination, and action on your part.

Now that you have read, *Parenting with an Attitude*, I encourage you to combine forces so to speak, with other like-minded parents. Some famous person once suggested that it takes an entire village to raise a child. I am not sure it takes an entire village, but having the help and encouragement of a few other parents can be of great help, even to the best of parents. As a way of doing this, I encourage you to find other parents who value and share your goals and objectives, and then begin to meet on a regular basis to support, challenge, and encourage each other.

One more suggestion if I may: I encourage you to use this book and the discussion questions found at the end of each of the 21 questions as a communication tool of sorts. In addition to discussing your parenting attitudes with each other, use the questions to stimulate conversation about what life was like for you as a child, and how your parents raised you. Then look for ways you have been influenced and affected, both positively and negatively, not only in your relationship with your spouse or partner, but with your kids as well.

For instance, read Chapter 1, and ask the question: "What did I hear my parents say about me when I was a child?" Using the second chapter in the same way, talk about whether or not you grew up feeling respected by your parents. Addressing your own childhood with each other and sharing how you were raised might not only help strengthen your parenting skills, but also your relationship with others.

Hopefully, as a result of having read this book, you have increased the likelihood of raising healthy kids who will grow up free of the kind of anger and self-doubt that plague so many adults in our world today.

Being a parent is difficult at times, and it calls for lots of wise, educated, trial and error on your part. But make it a habit to remind yourself that your kids simply do not need perfect parents, and that it does not require perfection to succeed at the difficult and challenging task of raising healthy and angry-free kids. It does, however, require that you strive to be the very best parent you can possibly be. It is my hope that by having read this book, you have increased the prospects of doing just that!

You have read here and considered 21 questions that I believe to be foundational to so many other issues that you will face as a parent. It is my hope that these questions have helped you evaluate and identify specifically what you can do to be the best parent you can possibly be!

Happy parenting!

Ed Wimberly, Ph.D.
raisinggreatkids.com | edwim@aol.com